0

Differences

of

Opinion

Bel Mooney

ffRobson Books

Acknowledgements   I am grateful to the editors of the *Sunday Times*, *The Times*, the *Guardian*, *The Spectator* and the *New Statesman* for permission to reprint articles that first appeared in those papers; also to IPC magazines for the articles from *Nova*. Jeremy Robson suggested the collection, and my editor Susan Rea gave good advice. I want also to acknowledge two special debts of gratitude. The first is to Anthony Howard who, as the then editor of the *New Statesman*, encouraged me (as he did so many young writers) at the beginning of my career, and gave me a freedom I have not had since. The second is to Jonathan Dimbleby, my first, best and most critical editor.

A note on the text   Often sub-editors are forced to make cuts because of the pressure of space; where I felt a train of thought was rudely interrupted I have restored edits. I have also added tiny points of explanations within the text where necessary, as well as afterwards.

FIRST PUBLISHED IN GREAT BRITAIN IN 1984 BY ROBSON BOOKS LTD., BOLSOVER HOUSE, 5–6 CLIPSTONE STREET, LONDON W1P 7EB. COPYRIGHT © 1984 BEL MOONEY

British Library Cataloguing in Publication Data

Mooney, Bel
    Differences of opinion.
    1. Great Britain – Social life and customs
    I. Title
    941.085′ 0924   DA588

    ISBN 0-86051-264-9

Typeset by Preface Ltd, Salisbury Wilts
Printed in Great Britain by Biddles Ltd, Guildford

CONTENTS

for Kitty
and for
Suzanne Lowry

LETTER TO THE EDITOR of *The Freewoman*

Madam, I once edited a woman's page (for a week), so I can give people advice as to how to use up odd scraps of macaroni, velveteen, and biscuit tins, and how to play the fool by painting drainpipes and milking stools.

Rebecca West. August 1912

Introduction

Hot Metal v Cool Mettle

It is, as Marje Proops wisely used to tell me, destined to wrap tomorrow's chips. Yet such a realistic approach to journalism might mean indifference as well as modesty: an attitude which says that since none of it lasts none of it matters. Yet journalism can last. Some of yesterday's pieces are social history and may be excavated as such; others are cut out and kept by faithful readers; many are referred to in cuttings libraries by other journalists. It is with amazement, not pride, that I look back on the hundreds of thousands of words of free-lance journalism I have produced in fifteen years. It appeared in ten glossy magazines, eight national newspapers, four weeklies and two colour supplements. Some was rubbish, some was good, but the retrospective exercise is salutary. You see how the world has shifted, although its social problems never go away. Your own opinions may differ now from what they were; at the same time the important differences of opinion go on being discussed. Deliberately I start with Mrs Thatcher in 1972: I was a beginner and she was on the beginner slopes of real power. The piece is both an interesting glimpse of the past, and a tribute to the great magazine *Nova* which was unique in giving its writers their head.

Experience brings facility. Cyril Connolly was neither the first nor the last master of the craft to warn writers: 'By degrees the flippancy of journalism will become a habit and the pleasure of being paid on the nail, and more especially, of being praised on the nail, grow indispensable.' Fifteen years' freelancing means you can turn many tricks, like the most skilled Soho practitioner of that other profession. I am glad to have written for the *Morning Star* as well as the *Telegraph Magazine*; to have advised *Cosmopolitan* readers how to improve sex, and also educated takers of the *New Statesman* in the complexities of the parole system or the wastefulness of the Ministry of Defence. Being pigeon-holed (the bane of good writers) I avoided – or so I thought. No doubt the plump pigeon deceives itself as to the nature of freedom, sitting on the perch with the door closed, but the birdseed still coming.

So let me cast self-deception aside. This is a collection of articles that were not written for women, although some appeared on pages 'for' women, and yet I am a 'women's journalist': typeset, typecast, typed. That is not a complaint, it is a description. But the attractive label sticks a writer (or editor) immediately on the supermarket shelf, next to the instant meals. Rather than apologize for reprinting ephemera, I take the chance instead to examine the label, and analyse what effect it has on the purchaser and on the product itself.

This selection is varied, but I should start with a confession: left out of it are pieces I am ashamed to have written. This for example:

> If I were a blonde I'd be angry right now. Because according to one determined businesswoman blondes just cannot get ahead. A lady called Prue Warne set up a company of steel stockbrokers in the West Midlands and discovered that orders were sparse. She thought it was simply because men could not take her seriously – chatting her up as a dizzy blonde instead of treating her as the boss. So off she went to the hairdresser, and had those shoulder-length tresses trimmed, and the neat crop dyed a sensible brown. Now, according to Prue, business is booming and she puts it all down to her new look. Men, it seems, think blondes are dumb.

And well they might, if that is the sort of stuff blondes like to read over breakfast. There is nothing wrong with the style, but the subject matter itself confirms all the prejudices about women held by the average tabloid editor and reader. I hasten to add that the 'idea' was not mine; the fact that I was told to write it and that I did is a neat encapsulation of the woman columnist's role, as seen by the men who employ her. When I was a *Daily Mirror* columnist I wrote more words about a starlet called Britt Ekland than I would have dreamed possible. The executives were convinced that miners' wives in Barnsley shared their own prurient fascination with showbiz scandals. Protests were greeted by advice not to be 'hectoring' or 'on a soapbox'. Soap flakes – yes; no soap box, and definitely no politics.

Most readers would be amazed at the fatuous rubbish competent women have to take from the jolly but ill-educated office boys and businessmen who rise to run Fleet Street. Once a senior executive told me reverently, 'The *Mirror* is a golden ball you hold in your hands.' (This was alarming; where was the other one?) 'What happens if I drop it?' I asked. He glanced complacently at his two colleagues. 'One of us will pick it up and put it right back.' I sighed with relief. Those men were being perfectly agreeable, and were in fact pleasanter than average specimens of *homo editans*. Yet the scene was symbolic: puppet masters dangle poor Judy who must never deviate from her preordained role in Punch's old show. The role is limiting; I believe that women will never dig their heels into the power structures of newspapers until the ghetto of 'women's journalism' is forever abolished. Since words were first set into hot metal, the men who dominate the trade have persistently underestimated the mettle of the women who should have shared their power. That this is demeaning for the women is unarguable. That it has a damaging effect on the quality of our Press is actually far more important.

It is not just a down-market trait. When the distinguished Frank Giles, then editor of the *Sunday Times*, interviewed me for the job of 'woman columnist' on his paper, he began by asking penetratingly, 'How are you on feminism?' I should have replied, 'Oh, feminism is the most significant social change of the nineteenth and twentieth centuries, and has altered for the better the lives even of women who abhor its ideas.' I should have asked, 'How are *you* on feminism?' But his question required only one response: a denial as the cock crew. And so I muttered something non-commital. That is the measure of Fleet Street's anti-feminism, or (more precisely) its complete ignorance of what it means: working in that man's world you are turned into a dissembler.

Now, the question was motivated by hostility towards an idea. The hostility stems from atavistic fantasies about what women are like, and a terrified dislike of any shift away from that dimly-conceived ideal. Over expense-account lunches the newspaper executives and their bosses dream of fair women; they are (with some noble exceptions) chicken-and-champagne cowboys who would turn all of us into housewives or whores. This fantasy, in turn, derives from an imperfect knowledge of who the female readers of newspapers are, let alone what they want to read; an ignorance shared by those who handle advertising accounts and women's magazines. There is an inescapable connexion between the lack of proper opportunity for women within newspapers, and the scant respect shown to the women who read those newspapers, and the false stereotypes of women peddled by those whose advertisements give newspapers necessary income. It is the tabloid 'models 'n mums' packaging which refuses to acknowledge the independence, courage, resourcefulness and intelligence of half the population. Talk to the average deputy editor for ten minutes about the women's page content, and it soon becomes clear that his ideal reader is a bargain-basement Beatrice, ready to lead her man ever upwards in the quest for a material *Paradiso*.

There is nothing new in the dichotomy; it was described in the last decade of the nineteenth century by T. H. Huxley: 'With few insignificant exceptions girls have been educated either to be drudges or toys beneath man; or a sort of angels above him . . . The possibility that the ideal of womanhood lies neither in the fair saint or the fair sinner, that women are meant neither to be men's guides nor their playthings, but their comrades, their fellows and their equals . . . does not seem to have entered into the minds of those who have had the conduct of the education of girls.' Nor has it yet penetrated the collective mentality of journalism. By under-estimating what female readers want, by not having the imagination to see that their needs go far beyond the slimming-sex-gossip-clothes-homespun-wisdom formula, the antediluvian hot metal merchants sell both readers and writers short. There is new technology in Fleet Street, but ideas are cast firmly in an ancient mould.

So it is logical that women journalists will be picked for an ability to serve up what the women readers are supposed to want. In 1972 Tom Baistow wrote a good piece in the *New Statesman*, called 'Ladies of the Street', which compared the style of Lynda Lee Potter and Jean Rook (good professionals both) with *Private Eye*'s brilliant parody, Glenda Slag. He found little difference between them, and went on to marvel at the obdurate stupidity of some newspaper moguls:

> The pop papers' fault is not simply that they compartmentalize 'women's interests', but treat their women readers as if *la différence* put them on a lower intellectual plane. The fact is that women have played a serious part in journalism since the cigar-smoking Harriet Martineau wrote leaders for the *Daily News* in the 1860s and helped to swing Britain behind the North in the American Civil War. From my former colleague Norah Bowes, a redoubtable figure in Suffragette tweeds, to Clare Hollingworth, the *Telegraph*'s roving correspondent, they have been demonstrating to editors that they are at least as capable and intellectually qualified as their male colleagues. Yet they have never achieved equality as journalists or readers. My guess is that they won't until the last Miss Slag has passed on to the celestial heap.

To say that other names could now be added to Baistow's list is no counter-argument to his case. Of course there are excellent reporters, like Melanie Philips of the *Guardian*; special feature writers, like Anne Leslie, of the *Daily Mail*; literary editors like Claire Tomalin of the *Sunday Times*, and assistant editors like Ann Robinson of the *Daily Mirror*. The very fact that the names spring to mind as isolated examples is evidence in itself; whilst there are one or two others who have an executive title, but no executive role. What is more, the numbers are diminishing. Last year Felicity Green, a tough and able woman who was the first to be tipped as a potential future editor, was ignominiously and unjustly sacked when Sir Larry Lamb took over the ailing *Daily Express*. Significantly it never occurs to proprietors that a tottering paper needs the kind of radical approach women like Green would certainly bring to the Editor's chair, rather than the old formulae of a re-cycled page three boy.

The serious implication of Baistow's argument is that change will not occur until women stop accepting the roles they are given. But because there exists a ghetto called the 'women's page', the majority of talented writers and editors find themselves herded into it as into a cosy pink cul-de-sac. Then they are set into absurd and unfair competition against each other, because the space is so limited and the editorial role so narrowly defined. In October 1983 one of the cleverest and most able women in journalism was sacked from a quality newspaper, to make room for another woman (also experienced, though very different) who had been hired to make the women's pages 'more mainstream' – in other words, softer and more feminine. The point about that story is this: had the woman executive been male she would certainly not have been fired, but moved sideways to run a different department. She was not fired because of incompetence, but because (despite all her skill) she could only be fitted into one role. The insulting paucity of imagination is breathtaking.

The argument revolves around the symbol of the women's page. In the Seventies there was an internal debate at the *Guardian* which resulted in the substitution of 'Miscellany' for the women's page logo. It was a general features page, upon which you would logically find Jill Tweedie. Then came an interesting but inevitable backlash (corresponding, I think, to a movement of separatism in feminism) which demanded, 'Why *shouldn't* women have their own pages? If we don't, the chauvinist men who run newspapers won't give space to our kind of features.' There was some logic to it (because in 1975 the women's movement was at its height, the sex discrimination bill was going through, and women were making news) and the reborn 'Guardian Women' was excellent. Suzanne

Lowry wanted to develop 'a page written *by*, and *about*, but not *for*, women'; but sadly the name which has passed into the language has also given a licence to laugh at preoccupations that are not exclusively women's. Its proper time has passed. It seems to me that the only paper which got it right is *The Times* – with no women's pages as such, but excellent fashion coverage on one day, miscellaneous features on other days, and a deliberate 'humanizing' of its feature material without tagging irrelevant gender on to good journalism.

There are no 'women's subjects' in newspapers. There may be areas that interest women more (like fashion), but none that are exclusively feminine. Newspapers have two functions: the reporting of news and the coverage/analysis of ideas and trends. Under that last umbrella will shelter fashion and food because what we wear and what we eat are signs of the times; equally – writers like Bernard Levin and Jill Tweedie, for their acute intelligence, and Miles Kington and Jilly Cooper for their wit. Features are asexual: men divorce, worry about their children, examine the mirror for signs of age, hold strong views about abortion, are moved to tears and display an interest in the price of steak. To describe those as 'women's subjects' is an insult to men, as well as to the women who read the leading articles, the reviews, and the sports pages.

It all stems from a very old equation: woman equals emotion. In 1852 G. H. Lewes (Mr George Eliot) argued that women writers were 'better fitted to give expression to the emotional facts of life'. So – newspapers hire women like myself to spout frivolity or gentle wisdom about a tiny range of subjects, but woe betide you if you commit the cardinal sin of 'sounding like a leader'. With characteristic coolness Angela Carter makes short work of that cliché: 'In this most insulting mythic redefinition of myself, that of occult priestess, I am indeed allowed to speak but only of things that male society does not take seriously. I can hint at dreams, I can even personify the imagination, but that is only because I am not rational enough to cope with reality . . . All the mythic versions of women, from the myth of the redeeming purity of the virgin to that of reconciling mother, are consolatory nonsenses.' (*The Sadeian Women*)

It is ironic that in an age when women are marketing executives, scientists, engineers, doctors, philosophers and Prime Ministers, those 'nonsenses' are still embraced by a newspaper industry which is further away than ever from treating women with respect. The men who believe the nonsenses are the same men Rebecca West dismissed in 1913 as 'the dreary mob of Pecksniffs and heavy-jowled stockbrokers who stand behind these papers'. They are the ones who murmur hopefully of 'mainstream women', yet would not recognize one were she to leap from the water on to the plate and lie there covered with *sauce tartare*. If Rebecca West, the most brilliant journalist of this century, walked down Fleet Street today in search of work, you can be sure she would be questioned closely about her pernicious feminism, and advised to write from the woman's viewpoint, without sounding too opinionated.

The question to ask, finally, is not what irritation this causes women journalists, for they are a tolerant bunch; besides, I should not bother to argue the case for the sake of relatively few egos. Many women will accept the roles they are offered, others will move away to other fields; meanwhile the men will amuse themselves with talk of stridency, no matter how reasonably the case is put – and it was ever thus. Fleet Street, of course, will lumber on. Or will it? The really vital question is this: what effect does this atrophied atmosphere have on the newspapers themselves? The industry has only just awoken from a long hibernation to face the technological spring and, shaking itself sleepily, it faces extinction. Burgeoning television capabilities offer news and entertainment twice as quickly, and it is pointless for proprietors and editors to argue that only recalcitrant print unions stand between them and a new newspaper dawn. They themselves equal those unions in a sad lack of vision, of which out-of-date attitudes to women are only the symbol.

I happen to be a committed member of the breed which says that print *matters*, that a newspaper can offer of service (easily portable and cheap), of information, entertainment, comment and interpretation that television, no matter how various, can only attempt to parallel. But only if it displays imagination; only if it chooses to believe that the readership will not be so corrupted by cable that it wants 'worse', but instead so experienced in choice that it wants 'better'. No one can possibly know. To work towards the optimistic assumption might be idealistic; to accept the alternative would be to allow newspapers as we know them to die altogether.

If we accept that the product has to be improved to face increased competition, the dilemma is, how? Present solutions are usually old hat. If circulation falls they sack editors, or indulge in the kind of 'war' that bewilders readers, who may only see one newspaper and do not care a hoot about 'exclusives'. Or else they blast the television audience with hugely expensive advertisements about bingo and other bonanzas. It may work briefly; we know that in the long term it does nothing to increase circulation.

It may be that newspapers have to accept a lower circulation as a fact of modern life, just as we probably have to accept a lower standard of living. That being so, which people are still going to find newspaper-buying an essential habit? They will be individuals who prefer a paper to breakfast television, or people who like to pore over articles on sport, rather than wait for specific programmes – all those, in short, who like having something to *read*. The quality of newspapers will count all the more. After all, the manufacturers of cheap video games have found themselves deprived of the expected killing, since potential purchasers have shown an inconvenient power of discrimination. To snare this readership permanently the newspaper industry will have to weave some new threads.

The real rot at the heart of the old industry is (leaving the print unions aside) two-fold. First, an ossified managerial and editorial structure which precludes the growth of new ideas. Second, an indifference to the readership and its needs, an indifference that exists at the top as well as the bottom end of the market. That is where we return to the issue of women: symbol of die-hard prejudice now, and potential emblem of change.

Newspapers can only survive if they make full and imaginative use of the resources at their disposal, and that must include proper input from half the talent: women. They must also give careful thought to the actual (not the imagined) lives of half the purchasing-power of the nation, and half the readership: women. After all, women work, join trade unions, organize charities, write books, become economists, chemists and engineers, run businesses and rule nations – all far from the Fleet

17

Street stereotype. It is the measure of my own indoctrination that I felt momentarily surprised to walk into a successful young 'high tech' company, and find that the person running its total marketing operation is a woman of my own generation. In Fleet Street that would not happen, nor would talented women like Verity Lambert and Jo Sandilands (running Thorn EMI and Capital Radio respectively) have been given the chance to reach comparable positions.

The loss to newspapers is considerable, and it cannot continue. First, the subtle variety of women readers' lives has to be understood, respected and catered for. To that end (and the next) the woman's page has to go. When it goes, women writers will have a better chance of displaying the full range of their abilities, instead of being pushed into the ghetto – and they must take their chance in the market-place and be judged on talent alone. And when mettlesome women take their rightful places in the editorial chairs and in the boardrooms of Fleet Street, then the old school will sit weeping into their wine – mourning the passing of hot metal, and cosy warm women.

People

Thatcher in the Rye

(*Nova 1972*)

I did not really intend to see them as mini-Thatchers. But on this day, when Mrs Thatcher was making her visit, the prefects at Cobham Hall Independent School for Girls wore rosettes of the palest blue. In a semi-circle they sat, describing their good fortune. There were the magnificent surroundings to the gracious school, the small classes (only two or three in a group at A-level), the wide variety of subjects – and now the new sixth-form house, individual study bedrooms and all. That is why Mrs Thatcher is coming. The girls, their voices delicately pitched, their clothes well cut, confess to an interest in politics. The school encourages it, even to taking the *New Statesman*. But we should keep an open mind at our age, they say; it doesn't do to be dogmatic. I suggest that since they will be able to vote quite soon they might have an idea, just might . . .? Oh yes. Confidence swells. 'I would vote Conservative.' 'And so would I.' 'And I'.

The chorus grows. 'If you are privileged you are privileged; there is nothing you can do about it.' And what, after all, is the good of feeling guilty? No radical chic here. And then we consider some of those current problems: 'Oh, things won't change for a lot of people, the poor, for instance, because they are not prepared to make long-term sacrifices.'

But are we really different, they wonder, are we conscious of being from a different class from other people? They smile and say, yes, there are differences – though they don't mean you can't talk to those people. But, 'class is a question of common interest'; and they are taken aback to hear that Mrs Thatcher does not believe this. And girls, she comes from a very different background from yours, went to a different sort of school. Really? Politely amazed, the blue rosettes confess they know nothing about Mrs Thatcher's background. And in just a moment she will be here.

Girls, the Secretary of State for Education and Science in the government of Edward Heath was a grocer's daughter. She grew up in Lincolnshire amid the Tate and Lyle and the tins. Sometimes she would serve at the post office attached, watching the pensioners count out their weekly money. Each morning Margaret Hilda would leave Roberts the Grocers on the corner of the street and walk to Grantham Girls' High, satchel full of neat books, eyes straight ahead. Always glad to get to school, always pleased to store up the ticks, Margaret came from a home where books were loved, study encouraged. But life in Grantham was not cloistered. Apart from the pensioners' pittances, Margaret saw how other people lived. Just around the corner from the shop was a little street called Vere Court, filled with the smell of poverty, the misery of what she now calls 'slum dwellings'. Margaret saw what it was like. She saw how those children suffered, lived side by side with them (well, almost . . .), went to the same schools. And with that memory, she says, how can her enemies accuse her of not knowing how the poor live?

Politics played an important part in Margaret Roberts's upbringing, although she was not conscious of it at the time. Her father was on the local council as an Independent, and later became mayor. In the general election of 1935, when Margaret was only ten, she acted as 'a sort of runner' for the Conservative Party – blonde hair flying, eyes alight with the thrill of that competition. For the moment, however, there was the battle of school to win. The Secretary of State for Education and Science gets very irritated when people – all those knowing liberal educationists – come to her and say that this idea, or that idea, is new. Their ideas are not new. Mrs Thatcher saw them all put into practice at her own girls' high school, where 350 girls from a wide-ability range came each day to think, as well as to learn the traditional subjects she approves of.

'It was really the right balance between the formal and the informal. I am told now that academic children have no opportunity to learn domestic sciences, the crafts. And I say "Nonsense!" *I* had an academic education but for four years they were compulsory – one year's needlework, one year's laundry, third year needlework, fourth year cooking. And you got in budgeting as well, and you were taught nutrition – and that when you are doing cookery it mustn't only be how to bake rock cakes, shepherd's pie and Irish stew, but you must look to the nutrition of it. I remember very well being taught that Monday was wash-day and that you had better arrange a cold meal for Monday lunch time because you couldn't give your attention to wash-day and cook at the same time. All this was clear to me.' Many things about education became clear to Margaret Thatcher through her own education – it would be the yardstick she'd set against the world, the telescope through which she would view her subject.

After triumphs at school (she was head girl) she won a bursary to Somerville College, Oxford, to read natural science. She worked hard, but played hard too – University Conservative Association, long evenings with her friends discussing the possibilities of world government. Those were the days of high ideals; of flirtations with fellow Conservatives, over coffee; of reading Disraeli and Conservative historians like Herbert Agar late into the night. Such was the excitement of Oxford then, such the time spent in political activity of one sort or another, that Margaret forsook the laboratories once too often – and failed to get the expected 'first'.

Four years' chemical research, and then Margaret, at twenty-six, made her first foray into the competitive world of party politics. She contested Dartford and lost, but won the heart of businessman Denis Thatcher, ten years older than she, who gave her a lift back to London in his car. Presumably Denis – public school, Army, family business and 'an honest-to-God right-winger' (the description is proudly his own) – won the heart of Miss Roberts, though passion was carefully controlled: 'I had two elections to fight first.' But they married and Margaret read for the bar, specializing in a subject close to both their hearts: taxation. Two years after marriage they had convenient twins, a boy and a girl, and Margaret was really free to concentrate on politics.

When in 1959 she was elected MP for Finchley newspapers ran stories about how she managed with her two children, and adoringly quoted her views on finishing schools, on grooming, gardening and careers for girls. This was the Macmillan era, and in the House of Commons she was less sweet. She supported a proposal to bring back corporal punishment for young offenders, saying: 'In our desire for humanitarian reform we have lost sight of the purpose of the courts and the true aim of punishment.' Quickly Margaret Thatcher gained a reputation as a combative speaker, one who delighted in harrying the Opposition. She was honest and made no effort to be popular. She supported Duncan-Sandys (then Secretary of State for Commonwealth Relations) in his bid to toughen up immigration laws; an honest-to-God right-winger, in fact, like Denis, loved by the women of her party (if not by the cabinet) who saw her as their apotheosis: the best of new Tory England made good, a triumphant product of the selection system who had shown self-reliance and had succeeded.

So, living in an impressive half-timbered mansion in the country, with her rich and right-wing husband, with a nanny for the children, and a cleaner and a gardener, Mrs Thatcher could not understand the murmur of criticism that surrounded her every public utterance. Although she occasionally pointed to her background as an example to all, she grew irritated when, especially after she took over from Edward Boyle as Shadow Minister for Education in 1969, members of the Press took an interest in that background in an attempt to discover whence this new educationist derived her views. Mrs Thatcher is emphatic – very emphatic – that she is not conscious of class, but of people. But having lunch with a well-known education correspondent, a discussion on class happened suddenly among the napkins and silver. The education correspondent let it slip that his father had been a policeman. Mrs Thatcher dived at once: 'Oh, you are middle-class. How can you have left-wing views if you are middle-class?' The journalist protested that his father had earned £4 a week, but Mrs Thatcher would not let go. Even more delighted to learn that the man's father was now an education officer, she crowed: 'But you are middle-class. Now *my* grandfather was a railway porter.'

And then, when visiting a rough primary school where the children were doing an experiment with cheap metal spoons, Mrs Thatcher reminded the children that these spoons were of inferior metal, not like the silver ones they used at home. Stories like this abound – but pass Mrs Thatcher by. She believes that there is no real difference between herself and a poor woman from a working-class background. She thinks that class is something invented by self-conscious intellectuals and cynical journalists.

There are, needless to say, no working-class children at Cobham Hall where Mrs Thatcher is making her inspection, accompanied by Lady Emmet, a Mrs Money-Coutts, the school's matron, a Man from the Ministry in pin-striped suit, and various florid governors. The day before, she had groaned, 'Oh dear, I'll have to wear a hat – they'll expect it,' with genuine mock-boredom. But today, she is just right in the black coat and an emerald hat with an almost arrogant sweep to the brim. Definitely the opposite of Robin Hood, that hat – more of a statement than a question. Moreover she does not mind wearing that hat, you can see. The groan was genuine, yet today the hat is unmistakably there, and in between the certain knowledge that Mrs Thatcher will not break the rules.

In her room at the House, the evening before, Mrs Thatcher had been formally relaxed, quiet. Today her other public persona is brought into play – deepening the shade of her voice to an almost plummy gush. From classroom to classroom we sweep, looking at exercise books – 'What good girls! Nice tidy minds.' Then on, admiring, with only a moment's tension when the headmistress admits that the girls do not have cookery lessons. 'Oh, but they must learn about nutrition, must they not? It is so very important.' She returns to this subject, close to her heart, a moment later in the tuck shop: 'So they *dooo* learn to budget, that's good. And they must know something about nutrition if they don't buy too many sweets.' As we cross towards the Gilt Hall for lunch, one lady behind me murmurs: 'Mrs Thatcher is absolutely charming, don't you think?'

And that, I am afraid, is the truth. Mrs Thatcher is charming. In a famous interview Godfrey Winn once compared her to the Queen, whose birthday she shares. But he was not quite fair. Mrs Thatcher is more charming than the Queen, her handshake is firmer, her eye-gaze more sincere, her smile prettier. When you interview her, sharing the same sofa, she leans towards you earnestly, patting the seat occasionally, to make a point. Frequently she wags a finger and, like a sort of true-blue Mary McCarthy, punctuates her certainties with smiles. She has been compared before to a headmistress or a school prefect, and it seemed a cliché. But as I sat in her office – with her smiling and saying gently, 'Now look at it another way . . .' and explaining things carefully in the tone of one who has long ago made up her mind but is pretending that the proofs are still coming in – I felt like a schoolgirl again. The headmistress's study . . . that girls' grammar earnestness . . . the smile below the furrowed brow . . . and me feeling guilty for having *rotten* thoughts.

The press officer said with an air of world-weariness, as we walked to meet Mrs T: 'I suppose you'll have to ask her about school milk?' But Mrs Thatcher does not wait to be *asked* about her Department's cuts, in particular the plan to abolish free school milk for seven- to eleven-year-olds that earned her the title 'Thatcher-the-Milk-Snatcher'. She returns to these 'hot' issues again and again like some well-trained pigeon. It is a waste of time to discuss such things as school milk, even to say: 'Did you really think your plan that the children should bring money in envelopes, and those who were poor enough to qualify for free milk should take their money home again after the teacher has engaged in the pantomine of pretending to take it out . . . Did you really think it feasible, Mrs Thatcher?' Because she really did. She cannot understand all the fuss. Mrs Thatcher is not sensitive to class but to people's feelings, so she understood that children would not want to be singled out. And, she says, the plan is well worth the fuss – a saving of eight million pounds a year.

It is a waste of time to ask Mrs Thatcher these things in a brief interview because, despite some of her howlers, she is a good politician. And convinced. For one thing, she learned all about nutrition at Grantham Girls' High and because of that she sincerely believes the 'women of Britain' are 'fully capable of looking after the nutrition of their children', as she said in the House. *She* is, therefore *they* must be. What's more, Grantham gave her an even more professional, more academic, grounding in the subject, as I discovered:

Me: But do you accept the fact that a large number of children are *not* properly nourished?

Mrs T: I say that there is no evidence that a large number are not properly nourished. Indeed, we went into the nutrition reports very carefully. Nowhere could they produce evidence of undernourishment.

Me: But there was a survey done by a Professor Lynch . . .

Mrs T: *Not* examining the children. He did not report examples of malnutrition. None.

Me: So you haven't had evidence that . . .

Mrs T: None

Me: . . . satisfies you . . .

Mrs T: None. Indeed no. Indeed, I may also say that I'd have thought they [the Labour Party] would have thought of that before they abolished free milk for the over-elevens, without putting in free milk for medical cases; wouldn't you? Don't forget that if there is evidence of malnutrition, mine get free milk. If there is a danger of malnutrition. So that's how it's taken care of. (*She smiles and looks at the clock.*) I have a constituent – and I don't know if it's a wealthy one or not! – at six.

Game and set to Margaret Thatcher. Queen of the School.

Her emphasis on the democratic nature of her visitors is significant. Mrs Thatcher is always at pains to point out not only how often she visits the homes of the poor, but how she understands them. She insists she is not conscious of people's class, nor of their financial status. If you suggested that by admitting differences she would be taking a step towards realizing the causes of those differences – a step towards real understanding and, more important, respect – she would gaze in sincere disbelief and make you feel rotten again. After all,

there were the poor people in Grantham . . . And she rein-
forces her claim to understanding: 'I must admit that when I
come up against a mother who doesn't know where to turn,
because she has shoes to provide and food and everything else,
I think, well, my goodness, what do I worry about . . . On the
other hand there are people with quite a reasonable income
(and you and I have very reasonable incomes) in quite good
housing conditions (and you and I probably live in extremely
good housing conditions) who have still got worries. We've
still got problems.'

And indeed, we have. Mrs Thatcher does worry, turning
over and over on her Chelsea pillow, how she is going to meet
those fees at Harrow for her son Mark. Knowing this concern,
she understands how a mother feels when she has four children at school: when her husband is only earning about £20 a
week; when there are school uniforms to buy, and meals to
prepare, with prices rising daily, and now school meals at 12p
per day per child. She can even understand why the number
of those qualifying for free meals has increased, with dole
queues growing.

But Mrs Thatcher sees further than all this. Despite some
fantasies on the other side whose record seems to have stopped
on the refrain that a child from a poor home gets a poor start,
the Secretary of State for Education knows that poverty is only
one problem: the middle classes suffer just as much. It
explains another unpopular step she has taken in recent
months: increasing the subsidy to direct grant schools. This is
a measure she is less defensive about than milk; one at the core
of her Tory philosophy. It is not helping the rich . . . 'If you
look at the income scales you'll see. The example I gave in the
House of £1,500 a year, that is £30 a week – these people are
not rich. What I am trying to do is give people of very modest
means their freedom, so that they could go to some of the best
schools in the country even if they did not get a free place. It
brings within their range possibilities they couldn't otherwise
have thought of. But these are not rich! Nor, indeed, have I
turned to my opponents and said: "As an MP do you regard
yourself as rich?" They are benefited too, if they send their
children to direct grant schools – as indeed many Labour
members and ex-ministers have done.'

Again, she wins. The Labour supporter slinks off the court and cries in the changing room. Margaret Thatcher, whether she talks about school milk (Labour withdrew free milk for over-elevens); social service (Labour introduced prescription charges); public schools (the Labour Government ignored the recommendations of the Public Schools Commission that their charitable status should be withdrawn) or direct grants (waiving Principle for Pragmatism, socialists do send their kids to public and direct grant schools), has been given *carte blanche* by the failure of her opponents. Apparently lacking a coherent philosophy of education, she delightedly pounces upon opponents who have disregarded principles that should be the core of their actions, and have thrown those principles into disrepute. Needing to qualify her actions, she is pleased to point to those who also took backward steps without being honest about it, pulling out the stopper of credibility with a sad and disillusioning hiss.

Meanwhile, back at beautiful Cobham, it is time for the speeches.

'It is a pleasure,' Mrs T smiles, 'to come to a school and know that I have no financial responsibility for it . . .'. More applause, 'There are far too few people capable of starting something with nothing to build on . . .' (The Man from the Ministry slides down a fraction in his chair.) 'Often one is asked, What is education for? . . . Of course you will gain a good deal of knowledge and learn how to think, but education is as neutral a weapon as any other. It depends on the purpose to which you put it. You can compare education to a dress. The separate parts are the separate subjects. You sew the subjects together so that education becomes a whole. Education is different as dresses are different. The dress does not look particularly good on the coat-hanger. And education is not very good if it is left alone. What makes a difference to the dress is how one wears it. What makes the difference to education is how the person uses it . . .' This is amazingly enlightening . . . the lady beside me glances at her neighbour with a look that says, 'How can we possibly fail with a woman like Mrs Thatcher at the helm?' Or, at least, with her there to whisper in the ear of the man at the helm, if only Mr Heath would listen. But Mrs Thatcher is continuing: 'In a school like

29

this there are opportunities not always available in non-boarding schools. It is not to say that one would like everyone to be in a boarding school, but to recognize that there are things it can give, other schools cannot ... They will get a large appreciation of beauty ... and not only of beauty but the feeling that there is a sense of history ... All of this sounds very idealistic. We are shy of showing our beliefs, our idealism ...'

But we thought, Mrs Thatcher, that you believed in realities, not ideals. You said so. Or did you really mean that there are different sorts of reality? You seem to think this school in Kent is an ideal school. But go to an Education Priority Area and it becomes clear that realities must be considered. And hard cash. We have to save on school meals, we cannot afford free milk, we cannot rebuild crumbling secondary schools if we rebuild crumbling primary schools, we cannot provide nursery schools, or new school books. Reality is hard. Idealism, for Margaret Thatcher, is something to be indulged at a public school, on a beautiful day, where a nursery school is provided for the teachers' children, where no one is arguing, where no one smells, where lunch was excellent, and where the servants had not neglected to give that little extra buff to the silver – on the day when Margaret Thatcher was making her visit.

In Finchley, the leafy London suburb she has represented since 1959, they appreciate that Margaret Thatcher is behind them. There, according to the party agent, she works tirelessly, seeing constituents, hearing their problems and only showing that nature of steel if she is kept waiting. There is an almost crusading zeal in the Finchley office: the agent leans across the table and confides, 'I would rather help someone who is *not* one of our people because, let's be frank, this may help the Cause more than anything. They go home and talk to their neighbours and say, "Mrs Thatcher is lovely and helps me". That is what we want people to think. That is what we are here for.' Considering Mrs Thatcher herself, he becomes even more fervent: 'She is a very good Conservative. She believes in the best. She got on through the grammar-school system. That is why she is so keen on it.'

In her insistence upon facts, her imperviousness to argument, Mrs Thatcher frequently shows the pious lack of imagination of the grammar-school swot. In her persistently contradictory assertions – such as that local education authorities should have the freedom to choose whether or not they go comprehensive, then a deliberate curtailment of that freedom in two cases – she shows a disturbing inward-looking blindness. It is not hard to see the connection with her extraordinary denial that class plays any part in English life, let alone politics. If you come from a lower-middle-class background, even more if your grandparents were working-class, like Mrs Thatcher's, you are inevitably, unavoidably, on the ladder of the British class system. Your parents had few opportunities but took advantage of what they had; you went a step further.

With some people this climbing up the ladder leaves a chip on the shoulder, an over-consciousness of class and a shiver of radical guilt. With some, like Margaret Thatcher, it leaves a kind of numbness, a denial that there was even a fight, or that it is at all hard to change your way of life and 'make good'. But suppressed class-consciousness shows in the breadth of the experience you claim. You understand the working class because your roots were there; the middle class because you lived with it, went to school with it; and the upper class because it is now your life-style. Experiencing all, you deny differences; denying these nuances you understand nothing. That is where we find the Secretary of State for Education and Science. And in that she has experienced a process of change in her life which she uses to justify her views, she is at the centre of British experience. As Mrs Thatcher herself once said: 'How we view the prospect must vary according to where we stand, and where we stand is a consequence of the way we have come.'

As a Tory woman Margaret Thatcher has been caricatured – an inevitable over-simplification. Not slightly scruffy, not Northern-tough, not ageing, not fluffy, not vulgar, like some lady MPs, Mrs T is well-groomed, well-spoken, ostensibly well-meaning, and well-heeled; just what we like our leaders to be. She is not confused by guilt, like Keith Joseph, but steams on with a self-confidence the British envy: a presence with which they can identify. Every Middle England dad, seeing his favourite daughter slogging away at her Latin and

French homework, girls' grammar school tie still in place, hopes that one day she will become, not powerful, but well-married and sophisticated, with just that little bit of class – like Mrs Thatcher. Even her tastes are satisfyingly 'middle': lamb and peas, gardening, the Black and White Minstrel show.

But though we may understand Mrs Thatcher, there is her role to consider. She is sitting in her room at the House, working out her policies, with Education in her charge – clever, very able and very charming. True, she has embarked upon a massive primary-school improvement programme, and is brilliant at extracting money for Education from the Treasury. To her credit, she is committed to raising the school-leaving age, though many on both sides of the educational/political fence would disagree with this. But education in this country is structured as society itself is structured, and Mrs Thatcher's refusal to 'see' the latter accompanies a negative and damaging acceptance of the former. And she is tightening her defences daily so that those real views on education, on race, do not slip out; so that she makes no more silly mistakes over spoons and envelopes for cynical journalists to pounce on. It is not such an amusing vision.

You see, I keep picturing all these children playing some game in this big field of rye. And nobody's around – nobody big, I mean – except her. And she is standing on the edge of this cliff and she has to catch all the children and stop them from running over, if they can't see where they're going. But she only catches some of them. Only some of them. The rest fall over. And that's all she does all day, catch some of the children. And she is the Thatcher in the rye. I know it's crazy. But it makes me scared.

The rest, as they say, is history. Mrs Thatcher became leader of the Conservative party in 1975, not because she was the best candidate but because of a series of accidents. Clever and well-organized, she benefited from 'tactical' votes from the anti-Heath element, and the shambles of the Whitelaw campaign. With Edward Heath routed, Mrs Thatcher was able to move her party rightwards, and Britain thereby shifted inexorably towards the era of Selsdon Woman. Nobody would have predicted in 1972 that Margaret Thatcher would become the first woman Prime Minister (1979–83), still less that she would sweep into a further term of office. In her hour of victory she quoted St Francis of Assissi: '. . . Where there is doubt, may we bring faith; where there is despair, may we bring hope . . .' It is ironic to look back at 1972 and note how much worse things are now than they were then, and how little has been done to bring 'hope', especially to schoolchildren. Local authorities are no longer required to provide a meal of a certain nutritional value for all their schoolchildren. Meals that were around 10p in 1972 rose to 25p in 1979, and reached an average of 50p in 1983, while the government scrapped the national scheme of free school meals for families on low incomes. When I wrote the piece above, one or two colleagues said that perhaps I was 'too hard on her'; looking back I think I was very fair. Incidentally, phrases like 'radical chic' (that phenomenon of the fashionably leftist Sixties), and the use of the cult novel *The Catcher in the Rye* as a framework, place the article in its time. I could not now assume that readers would recognize my rewording of Salinger in that last paragraph.

Jonathan Miller—the
Universal Intellectual

(*New Statesman 1972*)

If only *Private Eye* in its regular send-up of 'Dr Jonathan', had
got it right about Jonathan Miller. But the amusing Mr Boswells, in his chronicles of the life and times of the learned
Doctor, is wrong in both time and type. Try a century later –
and who was it who might have described the Doctor thus?

> Our author's mind is (as he himself might express it)
> tangential. There is no subject on which he has not
> touched, none on which he has rested. With an under-
> standing fertile, subtle, expansive . . . beyond all living
> precedent, few traces of it will remain. He lends himself
> to all impressions alike; he gives up his mind and liberty
> of thought to none. He is a general lover of art and sci-
> ence and wedded to no one in particular.

It was Hazlitt, another dilettante, another seeker of unities,
who predicted Jonathan Miller, although that essay was really

about Coleridge. Consulted on an appropriate 'type' for himself, Dr Miller might have offered this with a suitably modest disclaimer. He sees himself as a nineteenth-century Coleridgean wanderer amongst ideas. Many of his twentieth-century contemporaries see him, the man a magazine once described as 'doctor, writer, actor, film director, theatre director, critic, cultural oracle, and universal man of the cultural scene', as a pretentious builder of dubious intellectual edifices, a poseur, an upstart who 'interprets' Shakespeare, a panel-game pundit. Some of the accusations choke to incoherence. 'But what,' asks Dr Miller, 'have I done to deserve the acrimony? Have I not invited more hostility than the volume of my errors justifies?'

The answer is 'yes' – but to find out where he went wrong Jonathan Miller's sparkling career must be traced, moving as it did, in three parts: from specific to general achievement, from praise to blame. From a standard, middle-class, professional/intellectual background (his father was an eminent psychiatrist; his mother a novelist and biographer), he went to St Paul's School, then won a scholarship to St John's College, Cambridge, where he read medicine and made his first stage appearance in the Footlights review. It was then that loving media attention first fell on the nineteen-year-old Miller: 'the English Danny Kaye', 'a long-limbed hank of a man', 'a brilliant new comedian'. The papers added in hushed tones that he really was eschewing show-biz, he was serious about studying to become a doctor.

After failing to get the expected first, he went as Goldsmith's scholar to University College Hospital, appeared occasionally on 'Tonight' to earn money; then, already disillusioned by the rigid hierarchy in the medical profession, agreed to go with 'Beyond the Fringe' to Edinburgh. That was success – and the trip to America with the show, and money, and people being glad to see him because he was famous, and television appearances, and universal popularity.

By 1961 Miller was already attracting public attention of a more acid variety. After all, there was something wrong with him, he was too . . . well . . . busy, too serious. There he was, when 'Beyond the Fringe' was in New York, going to lectures, studying neuro-psychiatry at a New York hospital, without the redeeming sweetness of a comedian who knows his place. When the announcement came that he was to replace Huw Wheldon for a series of 'Monitor', the public waited with interest to see what would happen to this uncomfortable prodigy. They were not disappointed. There was the doctor waltzing around with Susan Sontag (who bore a triple hubris in being American, intellectual and female), casually commenting on Andy Warhol and Dionne Warwick, curling up on a sofa, rumpling his hair and gesticulating as he talked and talked and talked. It was what several 'friends' had been waiting for – proof that Miller, who out-talked them at dinner parties, and was asked to pontificate more often, was a fraud, a fake, a pretentious nasty. Subsequent works confirmed their judgement: he imposed his interpretations on four Shakespeare plays, when everyone knows that Shakespeare wrote what he meant, and does not need all this intellectual interpretation. Then the BBC gave him £25,000 to play around with, so that he could ruin our nursery favourite *Alice in Wonderland*, with an idiosyncratic gloom of Victorian relatives. 'Why is it,' the people asked, 'that this man gets these favours, this attention?'

From being seen as a delightful novelty, with a comic talent, he has deteriorated into a Man for All Reasons, a trendy all-purpose intellectual, a writer and lecturer on everything under the sun. Saying that he hates publicity, he has 'appeared' on 'Desert Island Discs' and contributed a feature on his daily routine to *Vogue*. Implying that he feels there is something slightly vulgar about the whole enterprise, he still appears on television when asked. Admitting that it causes him weeks of nervous tension, he still accepts invitations to lecture on anything that interests him. Like all unselfconfident people, he can't resist it.

Surprisingly, Miller hates socializing, is embarrassed by formality. When filming for the BBC he shambles about apologetically, so that the sound man is apt to come up and tell you what a good chap he is, 'not like some'. But when he is entertaining the camera crew with the technicalities of the eye, you see how his mind is not altogether capable of making the imaginative leap to someone else's. He miscalculates how much they can remain absorbed in his own idiosyncratic ruminations. It is a fault and a virtue: a fault in that it shows a deficiency of tact; a virtue in that the thought process involved is not a performance. It absorbs him and carries a sincere momentum.

Miller's thought processes, expressed in conversation or prose, are easy to parody. He has been called 'an approximate thinker', 'unscholarly' and accused of having too many easy opinions. He admits he talks a lot on radio and television, but adds that he only discusses what he knows about and if that happens to be many subjects, it is not his fault. In part of his book on McLuhan, this tends to thicken into indigestible lists of reference; but he is equally capable of producing journalism of the simplest kind. Conversation is the most fertile soil for his kind of mind – from Proust to the curious effects of a heavy lunch, he holds forth: a mixture of extraordinary intelligence, wit and ridiculousness; sentences winding themselves up into similes and metaphors, springing off into the air of speculation, occasionally falling flat with a twitch of surprise if interrupted.

> On whatever question or author you speak he is prepared to take up the theme with advantage – from Peter Abelard down to Thomas More, from the subtlest metaphysic down to the politics of the Courier.

Hazlitt was right. His range of interests is genuinely wide: he wanders at will in arts and sciences – but here the flickers of doubt come. Was Hazlitt right about Coleridge when he compared his mind to that of Godwin? And could not the same structures be fairly applied to our Doctor?

> Mr Coleridge, by dissipating his (mind) and dallying with every subject by turns, has done nothing to justify to the world or to posterity, the high opinion which all who have ever heard him converse or known him intimately, with one accord entertain of him.

For the Spirit of the Age is not variety, and in that sense Miller is out of time. This is an era of specialization, of experts, of scientific precision and careful analysis in art and science alike. Miller, on the other hand, loves to switch from theatre to medicine to poetry, seeing connections between things. He admires nineteenth century figures like Darwin, who excelled in both 'cultures', and models himself on his father who, apart from being a psychiatrist, painted, sculpted and read widely. When not depressed, Miller lives in what might be described in his own phrase as an 'inconclusive euphoria', delighting in his own Coleridgean predilection for the 'swimmy associating world of the mind'.

The cries of dislike come precisely because Miller is nevertheless a figure of our time. In the nineteenth century, at the age of thirty-eight he might have been Every- (middle-class intellectual) man; now he is Someone – the victim of a process of media-izing peculiar to this century. It is a building-up, an over-exposure, a creation of people into fig-ures of fame and importance, when in a previous century they would only have been figures of interest to a small circle; and people of public note much later, when they had done enough, published enough, to warrant it. Jonathan Miller's contradic-tory position is that on the one hand he exists in a world that is totally serious and private: family life, a few close friends, and private study – he takes his lectureship in History of Medicine at University College London seriously, has been working for a long time on the book on nineteenth-century mesmerism, and prepared lectures, like his British Academy one on cen-sorship, that are positive and definitive contributions to public debate. But that work is also the bridge (and since the Doctor likes connections he must know this) into the other, very dif-ferent world – which started with the 'new Danny Kaye', the money, the flattery, the easy invitations to perform in public, in fact the primrose path to Pseuds' Corner. This path appeals to what Miller seeks to deny, with many a Muggeridgean-modest disclaimer. With one hand Dr Miller, like many people, accepts the goodies of fame, money, opportunity; with the other he attempts to ward off the Harpies that come too. It can't be done.

Whilst it is true to say that Miller (whose theatre and televi-sion productions and books have also been widely praised) has attracted more than his fair share of lampoon and criti-cism, it is also true to say that he has over-reacted to it. When he talks about his critics he tends to diminish himself by that certain querulousness of tone. Aware of his own false position, he dislikes having it pointed out by others. Whereas many media-men would be quite pleased to have a mention in *Private Eye*, let alone have a running series on 'The Life of Dr Jonathan by his devoted companion and amanuensis John Boswells', Miller is angry beyond all reason and, more, deeply and genuinely hurt by what is said, no matter how ridiculous the jest. He reacts in almost the same way to a cheap jibe as to a considered criticism, pondering reasons and motives quite beyond any significance they may have. 'Let them argue with me', he says, 'let them refute my ideas. The rules of the game are conjecture and refutation and I abide by those rules. But it is not in the rules to overturn the table and shout "Balls!" ' And he continues to sit at the table hoping, whilst the balls fly all around; feeling helpless as profiles are written; unable to offer so much as a cutting, a review or a book from his personal store in his own defence – for he keeps nothing. Not the behaviour of Johnsonian pomp.

Fame, says our Doctor, is being known by more people than you know, it is vulnerability. It is people refusing to believe that you are in fact charming, harmless, and good company, let alone that you have abilities that existed before you were media-ized. It is stares in supermarkets, satire and sycophancy. The age of television has perfected its most damaging aspects – but fame may also be timeless. And out of time, out of the age, Mr Hazlitt and Mr Boswells came together one day to discuss the phenomenon called Dr Jonathan Miller, the learned doctor to whom they had both shown friendship and from whom they had both withdrawn. After they had discoursed on his likeness to their respective contemporaries, Mr Hazlitt demanded of Mr Boswells, with his customary gusto, why he so regularly railed upon the Doctor with such tenacity and lowness of spirit. Mr Boswells, appearing somewhat discomfited, confessed that the Doctor had done him no harm, indeed he had often sat at his table, but that the vision of his face flickering in the corner of the parlour consumed his heart with envy and frustrated ambition. For Mr Boswells had achieved but little in his life and saw the Doctor as one who had in fact achieved much.

Jonathan Miller is one of those figures (and this piece was part of a series entitled 'Figures of our Time') who kept on popping up – in fact his 1983 bestseller was a pop-up book about the human body. In 1972 names like Susan Sontag and Andy Warhol evoked a certain intellectual *chic*, which one suspects, in retrospect, of chicanery. Yet Jonathan Miller survived to outshine his own icons; he is taken far more seriously now than he was in 1972 (despite his irritating habit of 'retiring' all the time) and some of his productions, like that of *Rigoletto* for the English National Opera, were of such brilliance that even habitually sniping critics were silenced. It seems to sum up Miller's breadth that he stopped being a Fellow in the History of Medicine at University College London in 1973, but became visiting Professor in the History of Drama at Westfield College in 1977.

Rhodes Boyson

(*Nova 1972*)

Who *is* Rhodes Boyson?

A man of realities. A man of facts and calculations . . .

But also.

> A big, loud man, with a stare and a metallic laugh. A man with a pervading appearance on him of being inflated like a balloon, and ready to start. A man who could never sufficiently vaunt himself a self-made man. A man who was always proclaiming through that brassy speaking-trumpet of a voice of his, his old ignorance and his old poverty. – (*Hard Times*)

Dickens would have loved Dr Rhodes Boyson. He would have taken him, in his natty suit and luxuriant sideburns, held him up to the light, added a touch here, exaggerated a bit there, and revealed him to the world as an original creation. Standing like a Mr Gradgrind, feet splayed, in his comprehensive school at Highbury Grove in London, ruling it, parcelling out

41

his time: a headmaster of facts and figures, full of the weighty moment of himself. Or in his study, writing endless letters to the newspapers about matters of education and public morality, castigating the poor, the idle, the failures and the feckless, mourning the days when God and History were on the side of the Right. Or even, like Mr Bounderby, revelling in his past deprivation against which his present achievements shine the more strongly, an example to all. A Character, we'd have said, closing the novel: a curious character of contradictions, a character we are forced to like – though his faults are plain, his views unpleasant.

His friends and his enemies alike call him unique. Rhodes Boyson first became known to a wider circle when he contributed to two of the notorious Black Papers on education, published in 1969 and 1970 – collections of amazing, amusing documents that attacked progressive primary school methods, egalitarianism, teachers, Harold Wilson and all. As always, Rhodes Boyson was to the front of the fight. At the 1970 election he was a Conservative candidate (unsuccessful) at Eccles in his native Lancashire; he writes articles on education for the *Daily Telegraph*; and he can always be relied on for an interesting and controversial view on any TV educational programme. 'I am an interesting person. I have a lot of opinions. I am a nineteenth-century radical Tory. I am a political outrider . . .' He likes to talk about himself.

When you first meet Rhodes Boyson you want to dislike him. His political and educational writings are full of words like 'idle', 'moral growth', 'freedom of the individual', 'personal pride': gusts of rhetoric attacking left-wing intellectuals. His appearance, too, is irritating: a dapper man, given to wearing sharp suits with purple shirts. His manner is blunt, his accent harsh. He sweeps through his school – a model comprehensive where he has been Head since 1966 – without knocking on classroom doors, clicking his fingers for a boy to leap up and open the door, shaking hands with each member of staff with an endearing Gallic enthusiasm. Once a convinced advocate of comprehensive education, he has recently begun to have grave doubts – but still runs his school like a cross between a public school and a modern factory. A well-known disciplinarian, he smiles at passing boys with shoulder-length hair; the sixth-form room is covered with *Penthouse* pin-ups. The first contradictions appear. In his study – smart-er than the average headmaster's, as he is more lively, more sophisticated – he clangs out references to God and morality as other men talk about the weather. He makes no secret of any of his views. 'The middle classes don't know what they are doing these days. I believe in the workers and I believe in the aristocracy; I hate the bloody bourgeois.'

He settles himself, jamming his thumbs in the pockets of his beautifully seamed, double-breasted waistcoat: 'The state is an enemy to me, a necessary enemy – it tries to run your life. The freedom of the individual is central to my thinking – each person should mind his own business and look after his own family, then we wouldn't need these millions of social workers. I hate do-gooders; I believe in service, not rights. There is no happiness in right ; there is happiness in freedom. But it is not the freedom the liberals talk about – freedom means growing to moral maturity. Man only becomes good in a moral sense when he is faced with a choice between good and evil and chooses good. The more the state decides for me, the more it makes me a moral pygmy. So we should do what we can for other people, but not too much. I do not believe in a classless society.'

In a sense, Rhodes Boyson owes his own success to the one or two tentative steps towards a classless society this century has taken. He sees himself as a Victorian (and does what he can to whitewash the appalling conditions people worked in during the Industrial Revolution), although, if he had lived then, he himself would have had little chance to escape from the grinding heat and noise of the cotton mill. His family was Lancashire working-class; his father a cotton spinner, socialist and Labour Alderman in Haslingden, where Boyson was born in 1925.

'I had an austere and lonely childhood. When I failed the eleven-plus I was sent to the local grammar school as a fee-paying pupil, though father could not afford the fees of nine pounds a year. I was not academic at all – it was a reaction against my father, for whom books were more important than anything. He was concerned with reforming the world . . . No, I don't think it was a happy life really: one went into a shell and did not contact other people. But the only time I was really aware of poverty was when I was the only one in the school not in uniform. That was bloody, was that. I think the fact that I am fond of dressing well now is a reaction.'

It was natural that Rhodes Boyson too, should become a socialist. After the Navy he got his degree in politics and modern history at Manchester and went into teaching. He believed firmly in comprehensive education, and became a Labour councillor in Haslingden. 'That was the beginning of the end . . . I represented a large council estate on one side and old cottages on the other. In the cottages the old-age pensioners were paying through their rates to subsidize the council tenants, many of whom were quite affluent. I raised this with the Labour party and it wasn't popular. Then I began to doubt all sorts of other things. I am not an intellectual who spends all his time thinking, but I had to think the whole thing out then, and disappeared from socialism. I left Haslingden; I was nothing. So I submerged myself in historical research, took my doctorate, then found my whole viewpoint had changed. Other people told me I was a Tory. They took me to the Tory party and got me in.'

As easy as that. When he discusses this change of heart, Rhodes Boyson is defiant. No, it did not give him any kind of emotional shock – it was damn silly that people in Haslingden thought him traitorous. 'One was very sorry to have to change one's mind, but one did it.' He had one regret: 'I am sorry my father will never hear me speak on a public platform, against questions. I am at my best then. But he doesn't think it would be right for the Labour party. He has the same loyalty to his people as I have.'

Rhodes Boyson's people are very important to him; he is always talking about them. The difficulty is finding out who they are. His working-class background is a flag he waves in the face of criticism, the asbestos that protects him from the reality of himself and his views. He loves Lancashire and visits his home frequently; he delights in the fact that he wore clogs, once suffered some hardship; he likes reading historical novels of Lancashire, or as he put it, 'anything which has a connexion with me.' Boyson identifies himself with a way of life which is no longer his.

44

Now he lunches at the House of Commons with MPs (friends and enemies) and enjoys the fact that in the daily newsletter at his school his comings and goings, his meetings with journalists, his TV appearances, his well-known visitors, are carefully recorded for all to see. An editorial director of the right-wing Constitutional Book Club which recently published an attack on the Welfare State called *Down With The Poor*, he says he still likes to eat 'a bloody meat pie' at 5 pm. A change in one's way of life is common – common too is the temptation to use one's past to justify a change in one's way of thinking; a change which is perhaps as much the result of present content.

The conservatism that is the result of Rhodes Boyson's great change of heart is muddled and romantic. Against the modern world of Hampstead intellectuals, egalitarians, bureaucrats, and social engineers, he sets a rosy past in which men of strength and vigour ruled the land, giving charity and growing in moral stature through this voluntary benevolence. It was a world in which the physical well-being of many depended on the moral growth of the few. The cotton-mill owner would open a school for which the workers had to pay, saying he would rather be considered parsimonious than deprive them of their independence. This, says Rhodes Boyson, is a good view. It is at the root of his own philosophy; the stand-on-your-own-two-feet-and-discourage-the-lame-ducks mentality, which talks in terms of incentive, reward, free enterprise, do-gooders.

Moral growth is no more difficult at certain levels of society, says Dr Boyson, children can grow up in poverty but this is not wrong, so long as they attain moral growth. Of course the struggle is hard, but life is hard – and all credit to them if they succeed as he did. And if they don't? Then they join the ranks of the idle and the failures, feeding off us through the taxes enforced by our freedom-limiting welfare state.

Rhodes Boyson admits that his view of life, though not his fundamental fear of losing freedom, is primitive. 'I oppose equally the power of the trades unions and the power of the state. The capitalism I believe in is where firms like Rolls-Royce are allowed to go bankrupt, the state should not prop them up. I believe that people should lead their own lives freely and in competition. We have to fight: life is one long gladiatorial contest. I never drink Carnation milk because they say it comes from bloody contented cows.'

Underneath that natty exterior, underneath the over-life-size, cardboard cut-out of a right-wing headmaster, is a fighter. There are moments when you see it rise: mention a left-wing, middle-class intellectual and his face will tighten. But mention the words love and compassion, point out that there is very little of them in his beliefs, and he will clang louder – hurt and angry that you should attempt to break through his veneer of brassy niceness. 'I don't know what love in your sense means, I am always suspicious of people who write about compassion. I always find that they have none in their personal lives. I deal with people as real people when I meet them. I would say that I get on with people better than anyone else I know. I like them as they are – I don't want to change them. One's immediate responsibility is to one's neighbours; the compassion industry starts a long way away.'

When he says he does not want to change the working class, it is true. But it seems another form of conservative sentimentality, rather than liberal affection. You have your road-mender, a man who represents the stalwart and individualistic spirit of Old England, who is content with the little he has and who is afraid of change, thought and black men. A man of many virtues, a man Rhodes Boyson would shake by the hand. This is the working Englishman he knows and understands. His hatred of trade unionism seems based more on a belief that the old stoicism of the worker has been replaced by a degrading sense of injustice, a carping selfishness, than on his dislike of large organizations. So all the good men have gone, we are sliding downhill, we are a third-rate nation, a race of moral pygmies.

The exception is Rhodes Boyson. He is the example he can hold up to the world – who started off at a disadvantage and made it. Why then cannot others do it? His egotism bestrides the world. When he talks about religion it is easy to imagine a Boyson God sitting up in his headmaster's study in the sky. Rhodes Boyson is a Methodist – primitive virtues again – and brings the same hellfire to the lay pulpit as he does to TV screen or public debate. 'If I say direct to God that I will do this, then, by God, I've got to do it.' His religion matters to him in that it gives security and a pattern to his life. 'I have decided that these are the values that matter for me, though I would not force them on anyone else. Freedom, loyalty, honesty, they are a part of my upbringing, a part of me. And I like it.' He roars with laughter. 'I like me. It's not a question of having to run away from myself. I never get depressed with myself. I find myself endlessly amusing. I am very often surprised by myself, astonished by the reserves of energy I can pull out when required. I am always ready for the big match. I say, praise God for the body and the brain I have been given. As soon as the whistle blows I am there. So I am very pleased with myself – and that is rather nice.'

There is something pleasing about the way Rhodes Boyson's certainties, his honest self-satisfactions, bang out into the room. The most annoying thing about him is that he is easy to like – he is the sum total of the egocentricity within us all. It is attractive because it seems quintessentially honest. When he shakes hands with the school staff and caretaker the friendliness, the desire for positive contact, is genuine. But Boyson is so much the picture of the honest self-made man, so much the blunt north-country headmaster, who will change his mind and make no bones about it, so much given to airing opinions at the least invitation, so much the type of loud, reactionary, sentimental, pessimistic, free-enterprise-loving, conservative – that you wonder what is real, what is honest?

Ask him if he is being honest and he side-steps like a ball-room dancer. Does he believe everything he writes, everything he says? 'Yes, though I am emotionally detached from it. I am always watching myself in action. A dichotomy – two parts.' He says that if he were ever to become an MP he would never speak on any issue he disagreed with – though he would naturally toe the party line. He believes in the rules and in personal integrity. 'My own opinion of myself matters more to me than anything else.' But the truth, like history, is flexible. You can use the facts to project whatever image you like upon the screen. The picture Rhodes Boyson chooses to show is jolly, honest, friendly, intelligent, likeable. It is down to earth – none of your posh intellectualizing, none of your highbrow stuff: a man for whom the height of creativity is a brass band.

He will leave an important council meeting (he is a Tory councillor for the London Borough of Waltham Forest) at 9.30 pm because he believes in early to bed; he is healthy, wealthy and wise. He is a man the man in the street would love, clap him on the back and say, 'He's done well has our Rhodes – and he'll still speak to you.' This is what he tells you; this is the picture you are forced to accept.

Yet his political views are not jolly, friendly or nice. If implemented they would form the most repressive right-wing state. His 'written' personality is cold and inflated – it expresses an almost vicious and desperate need to observe the status quo. No welfare state, no student grants, no Open University – he attacks on all sides. He welcomes advances like the increased price of school meals; says that those who oppose immigration do so on moral grounds because they wish to preserve the traditional unity of our society. All familiar conservative squibs, harmless perhaps if taken individually, but together appealing to what is fundamentally uncivilized in man. The fight is not clean, as Boyson would be the first to point out. His philosophy depends for its survival on what he calls 'the knife in the back' on the fact that there is nothing like unemployment to divide men. 'I believe there will be a swing to the views I am putting forward. Someday there will be a breakthrough and I think that what I say will help bring it about. I have done my job, I shall sleep content.'

When the Great Day comes Rhodes Boyson may have returned to the blackened Lancashire hills. He would not return to live there now, but will be buried there. 'I shall not be buried on foreign soil; I'll be put in a bloody box and taken up on the train.' Then he will lie in peace among the factories he does not have to work in. And when the Boyson God calls the day of right-wing reckoning, Dr Boyson will rise, will stride exultant through the satanic mills, smite the strikers and the poor, give to those he judges to be worthy, and grow enormous in moral stature, shouting to the world that he is, he really is, *nice*.

Naturally, Rhodes Boyson did not satisfy himself with the Headmaster's chair, nor with the role of mere councillor. In

1974 he ceased to be a councillor for Waltham Forest, and became instead the conservative Member of Parliament for Brent North. In 1979 he was made Parliamentary Under-Secretary of State in the Department of Education and Science (which must have been a home from home), but was moved by Mrs Thatcher in 1983, becoming Minister of State for Social Security. Looking back on all the things he said in 1972, that is not such a pretty thought.

One small point of honesty: when I wrote this piece I described the Black Papers on Education (collections of essays that attacked comprehensivization and lowering of standards) as 'amazing' and 'amusing'. Re-reading those documents now I find I am in agreement with ninety per cent of what was written.

Everyman's Comedian

(*New Statesman 1973*)

So Frankie Howerd said to me, he said, 'What do you do then?'

'I'm a freelance,' I said.

'Are you?' he said, raising his eyebrows, 'Any speciality?'

'Anything,' I said.

'Ooooh, you *naughty* girl,' he said.

But fair dooes, fair dooes, Frankie Howerd isn't what you'd call dirty-minded. It's just that you give him an inch and he takes a couple of hours . . . And wait a minute, don't doze off and I'll tell you something else – Frankie Howerd's not what he *seems* . . . No. A taxi driver once got out of his taxi and said, 'What're you looking so bleedin' miserable for? You're supposed to make us happy, make us HAPPY,' he said. Not that I'll say Frankie Howerd didn't make me feel happy – I'm generous, see. Frankie took a quick look . . . 'I can *see*,' he said.

Yes, they're coming thick and fast . . . but of course it's not like that. Despite the taxi drivers, and old ladies in the street who greet him with that famous 'Ooooh!' and a camp flick of the wrist, the contrived world of comedy does not spill over into every day, nor is Frankie Howerd a permanent clown. So let's have a bit of the other: Frankie Howerd sitting in the coolly elegant sitting room of his smart Kensington house, explaining himself without giving a thing away. He frowns thoughtfully, qualifying his statements, talking on and on without a smile in an effort to reach an approximation of his meaning. '. . . All entertainment is escapism; we have to open the windows of reality to let them escape. I deal in escapism, and I need it myself. Acting, creating these images is a means of expunging one's neuroses . . .' The lines of his face are flabby and sad; he covers his shyness with swift metaphor and analogy, as if fearing the personal questions a pause in conversation might bring. One of the best comedians of his generation, he is worried and insecure. It may be a cliché, but then, as Frankie says, you shouldn't try to analyse illusions.

Frankie is one of those entertainers who has been around for years but only fairly recently 'made it' – if that implies acceptance and admiration by the widest possible variety of people. He started in show business in 1944 after an inauspicious beginning when he was turned down even by an amateur talent show. Howerd came from a 'poor' background in York, and spent his days at an insurance desk dreaming of walking on stage alone. Army shows brought a chance to perform, and after the war Frankie made it to radio, quickly becoming a 'star'. In the late Fifties he had a bad time: no money, no work, 'Nobody wanted to know' – a fact which has made him all the more conscious of the precariousness of the profession, causing him to work doubly hard whilst the work is there. From the Sixties to today, to his current BBC2 'Show of the Week' series, Howerd has remained much the same, though perhaps his public has changed. Praised for his professionalism, Howerd has joined the ranks of entertainers whom it is fashionable to admire; now even the upper-middles can giggle at his particular brand of neo-music hall vulgarity and camp.

Howerd's professionalism shows during rehearsal. The church hall is small and draughty; the actors who will be appearing in his Ulster show wait for the 'star' to appear. He strides in, unsmiling, wearing an old macintosh over a crumpled suit, stripping off his jacket and tie to begin rehearsal: 'Right, let's start.' Underneath, the shirt bulges slightly over

Everyman's slightly swelling stomach. Howerd's energy is astonishing: he transforms the other actors, working at the same two (rather feeble) sketches all day, until the pace is fast, the intonations right, and you guffaw yet again at the most obvious double entendre. In between Howerd analyses, saying one sketch is two seconds too long, suggesting that an actress might deliver her lines in this way . . . and he always improves. Frowning with dissatisfaction, he sparkles for a moment when repeating a spontaneous ad lib he had thrown into the Cleopatra sketch: 'I always knew her asp would be her undoing . . . yes, that's not bad.' And at the end of the long day, when the others have long gone, Howerd is still there, leaning over the piano and bellowing his closing song with gusto.

That comedy must be worked at is central to his thinking – even a casual ad lib rehearsal is weighed and practised with seriousness. He will talk endlessly about details and technique: the lights must be exactly right; his suit has to be a warm colour; his facial expressions need modification for intimate TV, expansion for the stage; the sketches should be not a second too long. Talking about this he is at home, going as far as to kneel under a standard light to demonstrate the importance of light to his performance. But about the 'why', he is silent, saying that he wants to entertain, to please – that if he became self-conscious about what he does he could not do it so well. So Howerd gets embarrassed by writers who 'try to do in depth interviews about *me*'.

To respect that, to stick with Frankie not Francis, why should a few weak jokes and the happy accident of a comically mournful face make Howerd so popular? His performances are uneven; his material sometimes appalling. The answer lies not just in the quick professionalism, but *in* Frankie – in the stage persona he creates. He uses his audience as other comedians use the 'straight' man (Laurel and Hardy, Morecambe and Wise, Hancock and Sid James) – as a stooge, a foil and a confidante. He will comment on its laughter, notice with it that another actor is clumsy or forgetful, accuse it of misunderstanding his meaning, and above all insinuate himself into its sympathy. Constantly commenting on the action on stage, he skilfully moves between illusion and reality, joining

them across the footlights in their disbelief. All his manner-
isms – the confidential nod, the shocked 'ooh!', the rambling,
man-in-the-pub type repetition – these never vary, thus
achieving the expectation crucial to comedy. And the laugh.

Frankie Howerd is truly common – and the word is praise.
He plays the man who will never be a success, but is cheeky
enough to wheedle his way into people's affection – for they
are not that successful either. He is the man next door who'll
joke about the boss behind his back, but realize that the job is
too important to do it to his face – it's not cowardice, just
wisdom. He is the private, not the sergeant; the man down on
his luck who has to go to the Labour Exchange, but tries to
joke with the pompous clerk; he is *us*, not them. Where Hancock blustered with more dignity, occasionally verging on the
insufferable, Howerd has none. Nothing is left but cocky falli-
bility; if ever he plays a hero, it is a hero whose sword is limp.

Limp. The sexual allusions and double-meanings are a vital
part of this picture. They make Howerd Everyman's comedian, cutting across class barriers where the 'little man' might
not – since sexual apparati are common to all. People have
telephoned the BBC to complain, and his 'Whoops Bagdad'
series was given a late slot, presumably not considered family
fun. This upsets Howerd – he blames the repeats of *Up Pom-
peii*, and the fact that a new generation of TV viewers have
only ever seen him in a metaphorical toga, talking of tits. He
protests that he wants to appeal to 'the middle' . . . but this
'sexual' side of his humour is important. This Frankie Howerd
is an odd mixture of knowledge and innocence. In one sense
he is like a man in a pub who will not let you escape the
heaviness of his observation – the most innocent remark, 'I'm
putting on weight,' greeted with the leer, 'It's going to the
right points.' But the truthfulness of the Howerd image is that
such responses are often a correct reply to what was *in fact* said
– an eager reply to a subconscious direction of attention.
Howerd is wise enough to know that few remarks *are* innocent.
His humour is a speeded-up parody of sexual exchanges
which are universal, which occur as much as the debs' ball as
in the Working Men's Club.

But the innocence comes with Howerd's own distance from
all this. Sexual curiosity grows more insistent with experience

– but the experience is all with the audience. One moment he may be their balding, shambling middle-aged man who sees his virility recede with his hairline and develops a line in patter to compensate – the man who can at least raise a laugh. But then he turns and looks shocked – it's the audience, it's their minds. His technique panders to the vanity of their experience, leaving him in the middle – an image no woman would find a threat and one that would reassure most men. When Howerd says that he is tired of this, that he would like to do comedy that 'deals with modern life' and not just be thought a bawdy jokester, he underestimates himself and what he does. This humour is not the true escape he thinks it is – that is the childish business of farce. Frankie Howerd deals in pure comedy, he *does* come to terms with what he calls 'modern living', even if he is in a toga. In its commonness his humour comes to terms with what we need, what we are, and what we like to snigger at rather than admit.

Of course he's acting – but not quite. Perhaps this is where Frankie and Francis meet and merge: 'It may be true that there is a large part of *me* in what I do. I can only act within my own range . . . the persona dictates the part.' But the person dictates the persona. Howerd is curious about people – especially about their weaknesses. He says this helps him come to terms with his own: 'If you knew me longer, you might be surprised to find me . . . quite . . . a complex person.' But the half hour on TV is simple – more important than weakness or isolation or anxiety, though these sober undercurrents are as present on stage as in his sitting room. Laughter, though he slaves at it, is the simplest form of reassurance – you either get it, or you don't . . .

So are *you* getting it, now? (A quick nudge) 'Tsk,' Frankie would say, 'There she goes. You can't stop these people. You turn your back and it's a case of Up the *Statesman*.'

And I'd say to Frankie, I'm sorry, I'd say – you see, I'm always having trouble with my end.

Styles of comedy change, and the television audience is fickle, but Frankie Howerd is still a traditional name in British comedy, with a style that does not date because it was never really a fashion. So pantomime (which he does each year) may nod in the direction of the new by paying the latest beauty queen to kick her legs, or by substituting disco for the fairies' dance, yet the old stars like Jimmy Edwards and Howerd still trade on their *doubles entendres* and music hall still lives. In fact Howerd has proved himself cleverer than most, by not leaving it there. Despite career setbacks through illness, he took himself into the Eighties by appearing at the Colosseum in *Die Fledermaus*, and by recording *HMS Pinafore* for television. You have to rise to a challenge, he might say, and there we go again.

Familiar Figures

(*New Statesman 1976*)

THE ROADSWEEPER

In the recent heat half the cats in Camden dropped dead. Nobody noticed as, in quiet back alleys, in front of smart terraces, and on stifling main roads, they silently gave up the warm, furry ghost. Nobody noticed because, before the heat could hasten damage, before a fly could settle, the roadsweepers from the council cleared the corpses away. John Kennedy, roadsweeper for Camden for eight years, wrinkles his nose to show he thinks it's not a fit subject of conversation: 'Mind you, that's not so bad as when they're . . . mashed up. Mashed-up cats is the worst. That – that really upsets the public. So you have to throw something over them, and shovel them up quick as you can. I mean, it makes the children cry.'

From leafy Regent's Park the one-way traffic thunders along Parkway, past shops selling pottery and Chinese clothes, salami and cigarettes. The trattorias turf out their wasted tagliatelle; the pubs spew crisp bags, cigarette packets and cans. It is bedsitter land as well as a 'desirable' residential area – home of a mixed, floating population of Greeks, Iranians, Irish, West Indians and English middle class. Along the main road, round the corner to the messy Inverness Street market, and across past Albert Street's £60,000 freehold houses with foreign cars outside – it's all John Kennedy's patch. Fit at fifty-two, with blue-tattooed arms and tanned face, he steadily sweeps the pavements, not bothering too much about what he finds. Sometimes a shopkeeper will swirl his own dusty broom out to where John has freshly swept the street, but even then he does not care: 'I just go back and point out, politely, that he's breaking a by-law.'

John Kennedy did not set out to be a roadsweeper – 'Let's face it, it's not the sort of idea you'd have.' He worked for years as a chauffeur, driving for the 'gentry', like Mr Van der Mopp the diamond merchant, 'who treated you . . . well, I can't say as an equal . . . but as a human being'; and for the middle class who hired the limousine for functions, treating car and driver as one machine. After a period as a truck driver he came to Camden looking for a driving job. 'There wasn't any but the bloke said: "What about sweeping?" I said, "What do you do?" he said: "Sweep".' He'd seen them by the roadside, those men with brooms and barrows, and never noticed them – because after all, you do not. 'I thought it was a bit of a funny job – not the thing you'd want to tell people about. But I thought I'd try it for a while, and then I got hooked.'

The men at the Arlington Road Depot, Camden, maintain that the days of the 'roadsweeper-bogeyman' are over. There is a Jamaican who works with John whose mother used to warn him, when he was a lad in Kingston, that if he didn't work at his lessons and behave himself he would end up as a 'terrible roadsweeper in the gutter'. John's father would use the same, threatening image of disgrace. But according to John (a NUPE member) 'it's a reasonable sort of job – and one that's in demand, one you get quite educated people doing'. He takes home about £50 a week, after stoppages, for forty-five hours, including Saturday and Sunday morning.

For that, he arrives at the depot at 7 am, and unlocks the gate to the yard where his section of forty men keep their equipment. He has to check the barrows, see that each one has its broom and gloves, and distribute them to the waiting men.

57

Then he hands out the green plastic sacks they put the rubbish in, judging the number according to the dirtiness of the
patch each man works. Though most of them would like to,
they cannot actually start before 7.30 am sharp, since before
that they are not covered by the Council insurance. But at
7.30 am they are out on the streets, getting as much done
before the crowds throng the pavements, blocking long
brooms by their feet; before the traffic fumes build up and
delivery lorries force the small barrows to move on and on.

John Kennedy says it is the people he meets who make his
job enjoyable: stopping in the public lavatories to have an
illicit cup of tea with the attendants, talking to postmen,
milkmen and paper-sellers who are as familiar a street-sight as
he is, answering the halting questions of innumerable tourists,
chatting to shopkeepers. Years back he swept Euston Road in
boredom, until Thames Television opened its doors, pushing
'interesting people like Eamonn Andrews and Monty Mod-
lyn' into his sight. 'Once I met the man who actually owns
the whole lot – all that Euston Centre – Mr Levy. He said: "Do
you know how much this lot's worth? Forty million pounds."
Funny he should boast to a roadsweeper.'

The unpleasant side is obvious: stinking food outside
restaurants, bags of ancient refuse dumped in back alleys, the
occasional stained mattress. One day last summer the depot
received an urgent call saying there was a dead dog to dispose
of. 'I went round and there was this little old lady crying. It
was her dog. So I told her to go into the front room, because I
didn't want her to see me manhandling it into a sack – they
get so stiff and heavy. I mean, you've got to consider people's
feelings. I went in the back room, and she'd put the dog in its
basket and covered it up as if it was asleep, all peaceful. Well
. . . it must have been there over a week. And it was weather
like this. It was nothing like Revlon, I can tell you.'

The public too turn nasty, objecting to rubbish uncleared,
'treating you like dirt', asking 'what they pay their rates for'.
John Kennedy's attitude is resigned: 'What can I do? They
pay my wages. Anyway I feel sorry for them if all they can do is
take out their feelings on a roadsweeper. What's the point of
answering back? What should I do – go home and shout out of
the window at the man who sweeps *my* street?'

He is also resigned to what he calls his 'housing problem'. For years he has lived in half a condemned house in Marylebone with his wife and mother-in-law. The people in the other half have been rehoused because of the damp; the ownership of the property has changed three times since Christmas, though no one has visited it; they live in four rooms with an outside toilet for £4.50 a week. He wants to be rehoused by Camden, because he works there – but switching from one borough's housing list to another is almost impossible. The bureaucracy is frustrating, the house depressing, his wife unwell – but John puts up with it all with an air of surprise that you think he might complain; just glad, he says, to get to work.

A student, on a vacation job, walks past the depot, pushing a handcart to the dump behind. John comments that he 'tackles the job as if he was an ordinary fella'. Once John tried to take his own 'step up' by applying for a supervisor's post, a desk job. He was shortlisted, but lost it – advised by his boss to keep trying because he 'had it in him' to take that kind responsibility. He shrugs off disappointment; just points out with pride that one of the supervisors, a young smartly-dressed man, 'doesn't look as if he's been a sweeper at all'.

Old images die hard. There is quite a high accident rate among sweepers because drivers do not notice them. When it comes to a strike the dustmen come out, while the sweepers carry on 'because we don't have the same weight'. Certainly the passersby do not flicker an eyelid in John's direction as they hurry to Camden Town tube. 'That's how it is with this job. It has to be done, but nobody really notices you doing it.' A car backfires and he looks very serious: 'Mind you, me personally, I have to keep my head down. Anything could happen with a name like mine ... and anyway, Jackie wouldn't like it if she saw me doing this terrible low job, would she?'

THE MILKMAN

It is a grey and glassy hour, between 5 and 6 am, when the alarm clock's tick turns to a threat. No thud of traffic yet to

59

shake the trees. The milkman carries his crates into a small council block, noticing with distaste the dossers (young and old) who snore on doormats, oblivious of the bottles' clink. Doorsteps differ greatly on this round: middle-class houses with fresh white paint and brass letterboxes, unlit council stairs, scruffy student flats, the carpeted hallways of the expensive private flats that overlook Clapham Common. Five hundred and eighty-six homes, all served by the same milkman, wait for the morning delivery.

His name is Fred Farthing: milkman for over forty years. As the clocks of his customers tick, he performs his function with the same clockwork regularity – not lonely, not minding rain and snow, not wanting to talk, not noticing anything much. He concentrates on time; the five miles the milk float can run, and the minutes it takes him to pace up that path, leave a pint, back down and up the next path, leave two pints and six eggs, back down, across to the float, and so on. He calculates he walked about twenty-five miles a day. The only thing that halts this rotating progress, this automatic application, is accident. A woman waiting by her gate, who calls him, may mean that he forgets the two houses opposite which he normally visits first. It irritates him. And once a lift jammed in the private flats, shooting him past the first to the second floor. 'I automatically did the first-floor delivery up there, remembering the amounts, not noticing till the end.' Like the postman, the milkman regulates himself, so he can finish in good time.

Fred Farthing began his career at the age of ten, in 1921. 'We didn't have much money, and I was the eldest of four, so the extra money came in handy. So I used to meet the milkman at four in the morning, fog or snow, and help him with his round on the horse and cart till 6.30. Then I'd go home and do whatever jobs I had to do indoors, before going to school. I wasn't much good at school. And I'd work all day Saturday and Sunday, getting 1s 6d a week plus a pound of butter. That was a great luxury.'

People slip into their life's work without choosing – so at fourteen Fred left school to join the dairy as a delivery boy on a bicycle. Then he graduated to 'the servery'; getting the wide variety of groceries ('twice as much as we carry now') ready

60

for the milkmen to take on their rounds. Next he was out on the streets at last – pushing the small hand cart with huge iron wheels, walking from door to door, learning to memorize exact orders. During the war, in France with the Cameronians, he began to remember South London, and doorsteps, and think about a different job: 'Why go on being a milkman?' Still, he went back: 'There wasn't much else, and anyway I thought, it's not a bad job. In the open . . . and once you're out on the round you're your own master.'

In 1946 he moved to this round in Balham: for thirty years – same round, same houses, same stairs. Houses have been pulled down; grass disappeared; babies grown up, married and ordered milk for their own children. Fred Farthing is completely detached from what he does and where he functions. In his sixties, he is unable to remember anything interesting or unusual that has happened to him during that time. He thinks . . . 'There was once . . . I remember, I was putting my hand with five bottles – you carry one in each finger to save time – through the railings at the school. I dropped two down, when I saw this Alsatian bounding towards me. Because I had the other three bottles in it, I couldn't get my hand back fast enough. So he bit me. I've still got the scars. That's the only thing that's happened to me.' He says that there is only one real change he notices on the streets, apart from the traffic: 'They're so dirty now. They used to have a roadsweeper down here but now he's gone. They send the machine along, but it only goes past parked cars where the sweeper would go under them. You can't beat old ways.'

Fred Farthing gets up at 4 am. 'I go down, put the kettle on, and make porridge – summer and winter. And I take four halibut liver oil capsules, because you need that protection out in the open. After three cups of tea I leave home at 5 am, and get to work at 5.15. You have to load your own float with the crates, then get your cream, butter, chickens, and other stuff from the servery. I start delivery before 6 am, and try to finish by 12.30 – or 4 pm, on Friday and Saturday. I could start later, but I'd be home much later – it's up to me.'

For the seven-day week the milkman will average about £45-£50, working on a basic wage plus commission. 'You have to get rid of a certain amount of stuff before commission starts at 5p in £1. But you can't flog milk to people – they know what they want and that's it. Your money comes from suggesting they have butter or eggs or something. Most of the time I don't bother.' One year, though, he was star salesman at his depot – and it is that enterprising side of the job that appeals. 'It's like running your own small business without the responsibility. The books are checked, but basically its up to you what you make of the job.'

He calls his job 'brain work', though 'the public think of it as a cushy number. They don't know how much adding up you have to do, how much you have to remember. I wouldn't have wanted to do anything else really – except I think, if I'd concentrated at school, I'd liked to have studied to be a carpenter. That's a real skill . . . But I can't say I think about it. You don't. I mean, you've got to work, haven't you? You *have* to – so there's no point thinking about what you do. I've never been used to big money so I don't miss what I haven't had. I've always worked weekends, so I don't know no different. I *like* my job.'

Balham is inner-city suburbia, where families settle, and people have not yet learned the habit of picking up cartons from the 'deli' on the way home from work. Fred thinks the empty future of no whine of the milk float, no alarm-regular clink of bottles, will come. 'Now you get young men coming into the job who can't stick it. It shows in their work: they miss houses, or come later, or don't take away the empties. So people get fed up, and get their milk from the Paki shops that stay open late. So then they cut the rounds – and soon that'll happen all over. It won't make money to deliver.'

That is the way the bread went . . . and it seems to be all that worries Fred Farthing. He says that nothing affects him – not work, nor holidays, nor irritable drivers behind the float, nor the TGWU, of which he is a member, nor customers. Not even picking up unwashed bottles stinking with green mould, or finding twenty empties on the step of a lazy household. In the evening he watches television until about ten, when he looks at his watch and prepares for bed. The gold watch is inscribed on the back, commemorating the thirty years' 'loyal service' F. G. Farthing has given to United Dairies.

As others are setting their alarm clocks for 7.30 or 8, he

glances at the gold-coloured clock on the mantelpiece, ticking away the *forty* years' 'loyal service'. 'It don't mean much to me. I just got it last year at the Pensioners' Dinner and put it up there and that was it. The wife didn't say much. There's nothing to say. These things are handy as a reference though – I mean, if I want some HP, and they ask for a reference, I show them my watch as one. It shows I'm steady, but that's all. Funny how they always seem to give clocks and watches . . . and I haven't even finished my time.'

THE SHOP ASSISTANT

The Oxford Street stores do not allow you to talk to their staff – 'Only to department heads, and management – after all sales assistants can't talk about the store.' But about themselves? Puzzlement. 'They wouldn't want to – there's not much they could say,' was one reply. But D. H. Evans did not seem to think it was such an impossible notion: that one of those impeccable ladies in black or navy, who stand all day behind counters facing the spending public, could speak more than the familiar words 'Can I help you?'

Miss Campbell likes to help. She could be in any department, in any shop, at almost any time in the last twenty-five years – ageless, unnoticeable, with her sleek, cropped black hair, 'flyaway' glasses in pale blue, red lipstick, neat straight navy skirt, and navy pullover knitted at night in her flat in south London. She is shy to the point of terror – until she is behind her counter. Then she puts on her own persona, practising what she, just in her thirties, calls 'old-fashioned service' – missing servility by inches of expertise. At D. H. Evans she works in the lingerie department, selling both women, and men buying for women, the most intimate garments.

On the collar of her blouse the badges glint like her spectacles, evidence of the seven courses in corsetry she has taken with ease. That was in successive spring holidays, after she had left school at sixteen to work at Gamages. 'You couldn't take courses in work time like you can here, but I was so keen to learn that I gave up my holidays. My father always wanted

63

me to be a nurse, but when I was at school it was underwear that took my interest. And father used to say: "If you do a job, do it well." So I decided to work in a shop, and sell what really interests me.'

When Gamages was liquidated, after she had worked there for nine years, Miss Campbell felt that her world had crumbled: 'A big store like that . . . where I grew up. You think about it, and try to work out the reason for it all. It's tragic.' She was redundant on the Friday, was interviewed at D. H. Evans (where sales assistants' pay ranges from £36 to around £45, with experience) on the Saturday and started work on the Monday, six years ago.

Since then the routine has been exactly the same, alternating Mondays and Saturdays off, working till seven on Thursdays. She arrives at 8.30, and from 8.40 till 9 am dusts and tidies her counter and stock drawers. All day, punctuated by tea and lunch breaks in the heavily subsidized canteen, the assistants stand on habitually weary feet behind the glass counters that curve in a horseshoe, waiting for the customers.

'You can tell by looking at them what they're going to be like. Some are very shy – usually the older type of person. Then some will come with their husbands, and walk out of the fitting room half-naked, to see if he likes the bra. That makes me blush – I don't like it at all. Usually someone walks in, and looks around at the different assistants, wondering which of us to choose. You smile. You say, quietly: "Is there anything I can show you?" You mustn't rush them, you have to get round them slowly. Then you take stock out to show them – my golden rule is, no more than six items at a time. More than that confuses the customer. The vital thing is to get them in the fitting room. Then, I say, you've got them caged. You've got their confidence. Winning people's confidence, then sending them away pleased, is the most satisfying thing about the job.'

Once in the discreet fitting rooms, the world reveals its weakness to Miss Campbell. First comes vanity. 'Even the young girls ask for the wrong size bra, and get annoyed if you ask to measure them. A little girl came in and asked for a 32B. And she knew her size, thank you very much. I finally got her into a larger cup, a 32D. It looked really nice. Before that she'd been pushed up like a bolster – you could have rested a cup of tea on it! People are so vain. They ask for a girdle of a certain size, take it in the fitting room, and they can't get into it. They struggle and pull and puff, and when I come back I can see them panting, and the weals on the body – and they say: "I'll take it; it'll fit later; I've just had a big lunch." It can't be good for them, cramming themselves in. But you mustn't upset them. Stout people need help.'

Miss Campbell *does* like to help, though sometimes she quails: 'Once in the fitting room they will tell you things. Old ladies tell you about their husbands who've died, and if I see they're going to cry I change the subject, talk about the weather. Because it upsets me if they cry. Somehow it's so private in there they feel they can tell you almost anything, and sometimes it doesn't seem right . . . to know people's . . . *private* things. You see, you're like a nurse. You see their bodies – and sometimes, how can I put it, the . . . *aroma* . . . is awful. And you see what they're really like in other ways – you see all sorts.' She leans forward with excitement: 'I couldn't do another job ever. My heart's completely in fitting people, and serving them. And most of them are *so* nice.'

Even the men. Many customers in corsetry are men. They come in with their notes from their wives: small and timid men handing the sealed envelope to Miss Campbell, who opens it to read 'Size 46D bra and extra large girdle.' And the young men come in for presents for their girl friends. 'They always want frilly pants and a frilly bra. Frilly — it's always *frilly*. And usually they ask for something red. They seem to like bright colours; it must be . . . more interesting for . . . that side of things.' But apart from the brisk trade in masculine fantasies, especially at Christmas when the clichés reach the frothiest heights, there are other interested men from time to time. These Miss Campbell does not like. They sidle in, and walk around for ages, touching things. '*Handling* the lace,' she says. Sometimes they will approach the assistants, on the pretext of not knowing what to buy for a mythical wife, and ask questions. She purses her lips slightly: 'When they come right out and ask you what you yourself are wearing, you know the truth, and get rid of them as quickly as possible.' She shudders: 'I don't like that at *all*.'

Miss Campbell is conscious of her position. When the

scores of rich Arabs come, throwing wads of cash upon the counter 'as if it didn't matter', she is careful to take trouble with the often incomprehensible demands, only perhaps a shade regretful that they are not English. When customers are rude, especially in the hot weather, she smiles all the more. 'If they throw things at me, I just pick them up very slowly and carefully, to make them feel guilty. When they're difficult, you have to be extra nice. I just hold on to the parcel extra hard when I hand it to them, so that when they snatch it, it falls on the counter, and *they* have to pick it up. When you're paid to be a shop assistant you're paid to serve people. That's all. Not to get irritable, or show that *you* are tired and hot. It's the customers' money that pays you. The customer may not always be right, but you have to act as if she's right. Checking yourself, always being polite – the ability to do that is worth more than all these badges.'

On her second Saturday off, Miss Campbell will go to other stores. She will ask for things – horrified to notice unhelpfulness; that assistants actually sit *down* behind the counter, do not serve with a smile, even use Christian names. Miss Campbell, who thinks she will be at D. H. Evans until she retires, will never tolerate such familiarity. To her regular customers she is Miss Campbell, and always will be – whose whole heart is in fitting foundation garments; who sits contentedly alone in her flat at night, knitting woolly animals for the hospital, resting her feet.

These were part of a series; Anthony Howard's idea that I should write about the 'un-famous' for a change. I still believe that there are few things more fascinating than what people do, and how and why they do it. But this 'fly-on-the-wall' journalism is unfashionable now, and the television documentary-maker has taken it over.

Places

A Little Typhoid in Glasgow

(*New Statesman 1973*)

The Medical Officer of Health emphasized that there was nothing to make a fuss about. After all, three cases of typhoid do not constitute a serious outbreak, and the figure is well within the norm for Glasgow. In fact, last week's news item about typhoid in Glasgow did not attract excessive attention. A brother and sister, aged five and three, then a neighbour's child, also three, were taken to hospital, and typhoid was confirmed. Tests were taken of people in the area in an attempt to find a 'carrier' of that particular strain, food shops examined, swabs put down drains, sanitary inspectors sent round. Perfectly normal – but the friendly Medical Officer of Health showed a slight touch of defensiveness: 'This town is always put down as a city of dreadful slums . . .'

The story of how a germ called *salmonella typhi* somehow entered the systems of three Glasgow children lacks the unpredictability of a really good mystery. It took place in the

Bridgeton area where once thriving shopping streets are now boarded up, and where stretches of sad waste and rubble, loomed over by modern high-rise blocks, testify to the slow progress of Glasgow's great slum clearance/rehousing programme. The people in Bridgeton suffer unemployment and alcoholism, poverty and crime. Strathclyde Street, where the typhoid occurred, is slightly better than some of its neighbours. The old three-storey tenements, with one lavatory to each landing, shared by three or four families are ugly and broken-down from the outside, but inside they show the meticulous gay neatness with which overworked women often avert the creeping squalor and despair of appalling housing. But despite the attempts at bright decoration, the walls are damp, pipes leak, and the tenements are falling apart. Pools of filthy water turn the little barren patch behind the terrace to mud – and shortly before the two children from No. 44 and the little girl from No. 38 were taken to hospital, a horrified neighbour had seen them playing in this water and drinking it.

But we are jumping ahead – first it is necessary to explain why there was so much filthy water lying about, necessary to describe the sanitary arrangements in Strathclyde Street. The Department of Health and Social Security pamphlet on typhoid explains that 'During the half-century prior to 1930 there was a dramatic fall in the number of deaths due to typhoid and paratyphoid fevers, associated with improved water supplies, sanitation, and standards of hygiene generally'. In Strathclyde Street, ancient malfunctioning lavatories on each landing are shared by up to fifteen people. (DHSS pamphlet: 'Organisms find their way . . . into the intestine and are then excreted in the faeces.') Each flat has one cold-water tap for all the family washing and drinking. (DHSS pamphlet: 'Basic understanding of the principles of sanitation and sound personal hygiene is still the surest barrier against infection.') The drains in the buildings are so bad that in summer the smell is unbearable, and all year round they overflow in the gutters, and on to the patch at the rear where children play. Burst pipes are frequent, and frequently unrepaired for weeks. (DHSS pamphlet: 'In communities with low standards of sanitation water supplies are particularly liable to contamination.')

Before typhoid was confirmed in the first two children, the Bormans, who live at No. 44, there was a burst pipe at No. 38, causing the water to be switched off for a few days. No. 44 was unaffected, so people from the neighbouring tenements were going there with pans and kettles for water. This was quite common, the families were used to the inconvenience, used too, to the inevitable drop in the necessary 'personal hygiene'. What struck them as amusing was the speed with which the burst main pipe was mended and their water restored once the Borman children were found to have typhoid. Normally it would remain off for days, as one of the sanitary inspectors admitted: 'Quite frankly if it hadn't been for the typhoid, no one would have done anything about it – not so quickly. As it was we sent a plumber round right away.'

In a sense the authorities might be excused if they had taken a long time to send a plumber, because the houses in Strathclyde Street are theoretically nothing to do with them – that is, until the possibility of an epidemic arises. Nor are they 'condemned' as the television reports stated. They are hand-led by different agents or 'factors', to whom the tenants pay rent. Now the factor of No. 44 has abandoned it – an action that was taken a significant few days after the typhoid out-break. So all the inhabitants, including the parents of the Borman children, received a letter saying that, 'in view of inadequate income and vandalism in the tenement we have no alternative than to intimate our resignation as factors of the rented houses'. This move is common, in an area due for redevelopment, when it would cost at least £6,000 to improve properties that have been allowed to collapse. When this abdication of responsibility takes place, the building belongs to no one, until the corporation decides to condemn it. Until then, abandoned – and twenty-six-year-old Mrs Borman, who lives with her husband and four small children in one cramped room, said in a slightly puzzled way: 'It's funny, isn't it, that they can just abandon it, yet all these families are still living here?' Then she started to laugh: 'I suppose we're abandoned too.'

71

But No. 38, where the parents of the third typhoid case live, also with four children, also in one room, has not been abandoned. The tenents are still paying rent, despite the fact that every tenement in the row has identically bad facilities. Upstairs the Ballochs enjoy comparative luxury. They have two rooms for the four of them, for which they pay £1 a week. Mr Balloch is a labourer at a nearby steel works, and like his wife he has always lived in Bridgeton, always been satisfied with his way of life. But now resentment has whittled away at his resignation. 'The factor draws the rent but he never touches the building. If we ask him to mend things he just refuses. When you get a comparison flat you get a high rent, but you've got a bathroom and proper kitchen. You don't mind paying for that.'

Like the Bormans they have been on the housing list for about six years; like them they have refused new accommodation because it was on the outskirts of Glasgow, making (with heavily increased fares), a move economically impossible. For the jobs, though few, are still in the old parts near the city centre. Besides, like many others who leave the new 'schemes' to drink in the old pubs on a Friday night, they have an emotional resistance to leaving 'their' area. But the typhoid has worried them. 'Mind, there was plenty of warning that something like this would happen,' said Mr Balloch. 'My son there had gastro-enteritis when he was eighteen months and nearly died. The sanitary inspector told me it was caused by germs in bad drains, or else these terrible toilets . . .'

A place like Strathclyde Street, abandoned in fact by everyone, has a depressing effect on its inhabitants, despite the fact that they try to put pictures up on crumbling walls, and make sure the curtains (which they have to draw in the daytime because of the draught where the rotten window-frame will not close) are bright. Some of the old women, conditioned to scrub hopelessly on a Friday night, complain that the young women do not try, that they have let a street that used to be respectable 'go down'. Theirs is a philosophy of proud and resigned slavery which the younger women will not embrace. As Mrs Borman said: 'You sit here watching the telly and you see all those lovely homes in the adverts and you feel really fed up.' With an enticing, unreachable alternative thrust in their faces, it is not very hard to see why they feel like giving up, why dirt is allowed, at times, to conquer.

Not that dirt, or sewage leaking into the water main, or any of these things *necessarily* caused the typhoid which has made the people feel, momentarily, less abandoned. It could have been caused by contaminated food (the last big outbreak in Scotland was caused by contaminated corned beef from tins), or by someone carrying the bacteria from a holiday abroad. But nobody in Strathclyde Street had been abroad. The fact remains that the Medical Officer of Health said: 'Typhoid is usually associated with poor hygienic conditions . . . the families concerned are in the under-privileged group.' And in a sense that is the beginning and end of a story that is not, like the little typhoid outbreak, very special or unusual. Nobody is fussing, not the authorities nor the people of Bridgeton, because it *is* very predictable, and Glasgow must not be blamed. It could have happened anywhere – Liverpool, Birmingham, Manchester, Dublin. Any city. Any slum.

It is worth noting that in the course of writing articles like the above, I have exchanged many angry words with certain senior employees of City councils, whose job it is to bring about good public relations. They want you to praise their cities; they sit in (usually) expensively refurbished offices producing leaflets about the sights, and failing to ring journalists back when we request simple figures like the numbers on the housing list, or the unemployment rate. 'You're just trying to give Glasgow a bad name,' I was told. I have been back since, and the name is the same.

England, Whose England?

(*New Statesman 1974*)

1 THE VILLAGE

As the Squire, whose family have ruled Fenfield since 1750, reads the lesson, the wind howls across the Northumberland fells outside. Once, his father's word would have filled the tiny village church. Now the congregation consists of the Squire and his wife, the Rector's wife and daughter, the district nurse, and a tenant farmer on the Squire's estate who has a reputation, among his workers, for great meanness. 'We are all suffering from a shortage of bread and other foodstuffs,' smiles the Rector, 'but Jesus said, I am the Bread of Life. Whosoever shall come to me shall not go hungry.' The Squire nods approval.

The workers do not go to church. Returning to Fenfield Hall for his midday sherry, the Squire comments, with a mixture of asperity and nostalgia, on the evidence of change. But there are other changes too. Two days earlier he had astonished his employees on the estate – farm workers, wood-men, stonemasons. He had sent all the men under forty a letter which warned that owing to the present economic crisis, 'the disastrous year for beef', and the now looming threat of a wealth tax, the Squire might have to consider redundancies. It invited any man who was considering leaving to do so right away. Immediately a wind even colder than that which swept the desolate fell land disturbed the tiny, poor, but settled community. It brought with it fears that other workers in this part of England, where pits have closed, industries run down, and the young left school with no prospect of work, have lived with for years.

Over Sunday pints of Newcastle Brown in the village work-ing men's club, the farm workers argue. Union men and non-union men alike actually agree that the National Union of Agricultural and Allied Workers' present claim for a minimum of £35 a week is 'too much'. 'If the man canna pay, he canna pay.' But they disagree about the seriousness of the threat. Some say 'there's hard times coming' but cannot believe that times any harder can happen to them. Others sense that their last weapon has been taken from them. Because of low pay, men have been leaving the land from choice each year, causing the work-force to halve since the Fifties. But to have that choice removed, when unemployment in the North East runs at forty-one per cent above the national average . . . some of the men of Fenfield began to realize that deprivation has more to it than money; it is also a question of choice.

In Fenfield, as in villages on large estates, and communities of farm workers throughout England, life continues according to an ancient pattern. Though the village is only twenty-five miles from Newcastle, it is isolated both physically and psychologically: a handful of scattered cottages, a shop, a church, a club – and the magnificent Hall. Most of the villa-gers work on the Squire's estate – or for the new tenant far-mers who pay him rent, and pay their workers less than he does. All the cottages are 'tied': pleasant enough dwellings which most of the men like – until their wives remind them that repairs are rarely done; that they cannot move; that possible redundancy will mean leaving the house (with little chance of another) or staying to pay the Squire rent, with no chance of a job nearby. It is the women, too, who complain about wages – though poverty in such villages is not obvious. The workers will list their perks – free houses, milk, potatoes – without recognizing their own subsequent lack of freedom of action. They will boast of earning more than the minimum wage – without reckoning up the hours. And they will sigh 'A farm man's life is hard' – accepting, in the main, a hand-to-mouth existence alleviated only by the occasional luxury of a salmon poached from the neighbouring estate.

The thirty-seven-year-old stonemason who supports two children on just under £30 a week; the shepherd who has worked for eighteen years for the Squire and who has responsibility for 780 sheep and forty cows on 3,000 acres of desolate, dangerous fell for £32 a week; the twenty-year-old farm worker who works seven days a week for £22 – all would say that, though of course they would like more money, 'We should all pull together. If we were to do without rises the boss could get his head above water – and he'd see we were all right.' Their position defies ideological cliché: these workers accept conditions and wages their brothers in other industries would laugh at, and say with conviction: 'The Squire – he treats us as equals.'

In fact, village life is as feudal in its essence as ever before – the rigmarole of class continuing as surely as the ritual of birth and death. Of course, in obvious ways it is not what it used to be. The chauffeur, twenty years at the Hall, remembers: 'The old Squire was much tougher than this one. When he said "Jump!" by God, you jumped.' He reminisces with old Mrs Spicer, whose husband was butler at the Hall for forty years, working from 6 am till 9 pm, retiring at the age of eighty-two to die – and they call them 'the great days'. At Christmas, after tea in the servants' hall a bell would ring summoning them upstairs, where the Squire and his family waited by the tree. They would pull crackers, and the Squire would give each servant a present, then when the candle burnt down it was over and they would return to the kitchen.

'All different now,' they say with real regret. There are no longer servants at the Hall. Yet at Christmas each worker on the estate is given a brace of pheasant (shot by the Squire's friends and gamekeepers on a hunting, shooting weekend), and a hunk of beef from a fat bullock butchered specially for the occasion: 'We all stand in a row – most of us put ties on – and we each go forward in turn and shake the Squire's hand, and his Lady gives us the meat, wishing us a Merry Christmas.'

Of course, this is generous; of course they are grateful. But they do not see the significance of such gifts. The Squire will use such customs, and the free houses, as just cause for indignation at each fresh pay award, and take it as a personal slight that 'they get these thresholds, when *I* certainly don't'. At each election he will visit each one of those little cottages and tell the villagers that they must surely see what is good for them and for their England – and vote Tory. On polling day he will drive them down to vote. And – if only they knew it – he will confess to the visitor that he is partly glad to have sent those fateful letters. Pouring another sherry he remarks with odd vulgarity: 'I feel I've got them by the short hairs.' This then is a masochistic revenge for those pay claims and thresholds – and 'the death of Old England'. It is the fault of the Labour Government, the wealth tax – and the workers too: 'You wonder, you know, how many of them actually go and *vote* for this.'

Despite the actual beneficence of their boss, and their imagined indispensability, the workers of Fenfield must know that the only thing that stands between themselves and exploitation is the Squire's goodwill: 'He's a toff. The likes of him are kinder to the likes of us than are our own kind.' The workers are caught in a soft web of dependency. Ironically, what makes them happier than many other workers also makes them more disadvantaged: they feel involved with production and work for a boss they can see; yet that involvement and contact turns their rights into 'concessions' and 'favours', and puts them unavoidably into the subservient position of a hireling.

The traditional 'special relationship' between boss and worker – where they share as common interest the welfare of stock and crop – combines with poor wages and tied housing to yoke the farm worker to the land he does not own. On the one hand he loves the work – the cycles of seed-time and harvest, of lambing and market, which involves him completely where 'a car worker might have to screw four nuts as it passes him by'. On the other hand, his knowledge of his own expertise ('The Squire could never know those beasts like I know them') breeds its own secret bitterness. Those who know the land, who care for the animals through long hours and bad weather, reap none of the profits. So the stockman at Fenfield, after the customary expressions of loyalty, will add: 'If I had my time over I'd never look over a gate.'

The work ethos of Fenfield means that the one man out of work, and the poorest in the village, is quietly despised. Least dependent on the Squire, he was the only one who would criticize: 'Hard-up? And him with his Hall and his villa in Spain? To him it means a difference of thousands. To us it's 50p a week.' And he was the only one to know what unemployment, and real poverty, means in the countryside. Getting almost as much from the dole as he did from the Squire, he now has to pay £3 a week for that once-tied cottage. It leaves just over £17 for the family of three, and no perks. They have no transport to get to the nearest small town – which means that food bills from the Squire's village shop are higher than they would be in a supermarket. It also means he cannot find work. The twice-a-day country bus costs £9 for a monthly ticket, and precludes shift work or overtime. More trapped than ever, he says that if the others lose their jobs they will know the meaning of real hardship.

'Fenfield' is in fact a fictitious name for a real place. To name a village where each man is easily identifiable, and where it is understood that the Squire does not even approve of work-gossip in the pub, would be to put jobs at risk and disrupt village life. That is the measure of feudal England. The hardworking shepherd would not even dare to comment, with an almost painful awakening of political awareness: 'If the estate was broken up, and things got really hard for everybody, it might one day give them that know the land a chance to farm it for themselves.' He is the local NUAAW secretary, and believes that the Squire respects him. He may do so, but he smiles at the fact that a shepherd 'who can hardly read or write can be secretary of anything', and says that the union 'keeps the men in line.' Respect, in the end, goes up – not down.

So, encouraged by the Squire, the people of the village will, as they still do once every year, fill that church on Christmas Eve. They will listen to the platitudes about bread and blessings, forgetting that they are one of the lowest-paid, hardest-working, and essential groups in the land – that God has indeed 'blessed the Squire and his relations'. They will sit down contentedly to the Squire's beef on Christmas Day, and surely drink his health. And on Christmas afternoon, as always, they will leave his houses, to tend his animals on his land.

2 THE CITY

Do you remember the old days, when there were green fields all round – before they built the terraces and Tyneside flats? When Dad walked from Newcastle to South Shields for a job he did not get? And the lads would gather round the factory gates and shout 'Hey, mister, have ye any bait left?', scrabbling for scraps. The gaffer was a hard man . . . but they were good times, those. When a woman in the street had a baby the others would take her kids, clean her house, cook dinner for her man. It was canny.

'Barefoot days, when you and I were kids' – the song, which celebrated romantic poverty, was sung on Tyneside during the Depression by men and women who had neither shoes, nor food, nor jobs. They must have seen the irony. The barefoot days are over now – thanks to the welfare state. But in Benwell – in all the dying centres of Britain's cities – there will always be those who think the old days were better. We were poor, of course they'll say – but we are still poor. Then at least we knew what we were fighting, and what we were fighting for.

The old have seen it all. Mrs Simpson is eighty-four. She sits nervously in her Benwell flat, in Newcastle's poor West End, waiting to hear when and where she will be moved. She says she has nothing to tell about her life: 'I just worked hard, like everybody' – growing up in Benwell, watching it become a solid working-class community as William Armstrong's armaments factory spread along the Scotswood Road, and the little houses for his workers gradually crept in rows up the hill. Passing all the pubs – the Blast Furnace, the Hydraulic Crane – she would go off to work at Vickers Armstrong, where she scrubbed floors and her husband sweated at the furnace. Then, when the people were needed to make tanks for two world wars, Vickers had twenty thousand workers. It was the last time, in the West End, there were so many jobs.

Now there is work for only four thousand – and Mrs Simpson can no longer scrub floors. She sits at her window and sees change: the people gone, the streets demolished, new houses built. Her memories are of unity: neighbours, friendly societies, street parties, her husband telling her of the union's growing power at the works. Now she is alone in her house, with its outside toilet, cold water, and damp walls – waiting. 'There's no joy in Benwell now.'

The whole city has changed – like Liverpool, London, Sheffield and Glasgow – pulled into a new age. It has been transformed by the men like T. Dan Smith, who both understood some of its desperate needs, and needed – for the sake of their own image – to deny some of its truths. No cloth cap now, but office blocks, hotels, a super-modern civic centre, white-collar jobs, incentives. In the Sixties the planners and tycoons gave a 'new heart' to the city – though it had had one for generations. Money was spent, and industry was lured to the green fields all round by the promise of more. They made new towns: Washington, Peterlee, Cramlington, Killingworth. But in the inner city the men who had worked in heavy industry – the engineering men, the shipyard workers, and the unskilled – found there were fewer jobs than ever before. The expansion did provide jobs – in 'service' industries. But they were not jobs for them.

So in Benwell the pressures and problems proliferate. The young, with no quasi-sentimental memories, know only present deprivation: that sense of neglect experienced only by those brought up in an area for which nothing has been done, where one in six men are unemployed, where thirty-seven per cent of men are unskilled, where fifty per cent more people are on social security than the national figure.

On Benwell's edge is Noble Street. The sprawls of the Vickers works on one side, and St John's Cemetery on the other, sandwich these grim blocks of flats – like temples to Capital and the after-life, with no hope on this earth in between. For when you live in Noble Street, an estate built as a slum in 1959, you are pre-doomed. 'Problem families' you are called, by social workers and by the people up the road – who might have been put there and are glad they were not. The council neglect the holes in the roofs; the foul-smelling refuse chutes stay vandalized, the stairs unlit, the drains uncleaned. No shop will give you credit if you have a Noble Street address, no television company rent you a set, no coal men carry the coal to your top flat. You are branded with self-fulfilling prophecies of fecklessness and failure.

But a young family like the Hollands consider themselves 'respectable'. They would say they are unlucky. In fact they are caught in a web of change, of economic and social forces, which makes them powerless. In 1972 Pete Holland was working on a demolition job at Vickers. He fell thirty feet, hurt his back, could no longer do heavy work – and found, like many men, that light jobs were very badly paid. As a porter, car-park attendant, lift man, graveyard tidier, he was offered arond £20; unemployed he gets (with family allowance) £29 for his family of six. He has a choice between unemployment and those service jobs which offer no more independence. They pay less and the unions are weak or non-existent. The men are poorer and unprotected.

Then, forced to depend on the state, Pete Holland has to contend with its complexities. He finds that he is 'rent-stopped' by mistake, and has no idea how to protest. A worker from the local Community Development Project (which has done much to give Benwell people both advice and confidence) tells him that he can get extra grants for bedding and clothes. He didn't know. But at the tribunal he is humiliated and frustrated when they say his thin nylon jerkin counts as a winter coat and will keep out those bitter north-east winds. He and his wife (a Londoner whose parents knew the hardships of the East End) bake bread to save money, and spend hours at the Social Security office, picking through second-hand clothes for their children, to find those that look as good as new. And at Christmas this year, desperate for money to buy toys, they saw Barbara Castle award that extra £10 to widows and other 'deserving' poor. They – presumably thought by the government to be 'undeserving' – had to struggle as usual.

The Hollands care little for material comforts: they 'do all right' on that money, want no holidays or new furniture, complain less about prices than many a middle-class suburban housewife. What they do want is a house. But here again they are caught. They moved into Noble Street four years ago because it was all the council could offer them, and it was better than two damp, slug-infested rooms. But now in Noble Street they feel forgotten. They have been to the housing department and waited; they have waited; they have written letters and waited; looked at the brick wall through their window, keeping the children inside all day because there is nowhere for them to play, and waited. They have no chance of getting out in the next four years. 'But it's now we want the garden for them to play in. It will be too late in four years' time.'

Further up the hill, in North Benwell, Jack Warman is also unemployed. But while Pete Holland is worn down and acquiescent, the older man is angry. He is in his late fifties; 'retired' prematurely from the buses he had worked on for twenty-eight years, because his nerves could no longer stand the strain of driving in that chaotic redeveloped city centre. When he asked for a job in the garage he was called 'dead wood' by the manager, and pensioned off at £3 a week. He says he is like the miners, laid off as the pits around Tyneside were closed, 'walking round with nothing to do all day – just cast off after those years of work'. He was never militant, but he recognizes a truth: 'Whoever you work for – they don't respect you. We've been waiting for years for them to respect us. All they care about is keeping profits level.' He is proud that his son will never experience it. He went to university, has a professional job, has escaped.

For most of the kids from Benwell there is no escape. The lads who sing 'We hate the cockneys', twirling their black and white scarves as Fulham lose at St James Park, are brought up in the welfare state so do not starve. They can afford baggy trousers, fashionable boots, a ticket for an away match. The style of life is good; the chances are not. If you are brought up in Benwell you are one goal down in the first few minutes. In 1971 twenty-seven per cent of Newcastle children took free school meals – a higher figure than any other local authority. But in Benwell itself about sixty per cent of the children get free meals, and Noble Street kids often don't go to school at all. If CSEs are an indication of worth – as they are certainly a qualification for escape – then most Benwell teenagers are classed as hopeless before they leave school. And when they look for work . . . the web closes in again.

Two women sit talking at 'The Observer Place', an advice centre set up by the Benwell Action Group. They discuss their sons. One tells how her boy took a bricklaying apprenticeship when he left school. After two years, before he had finished, the firm went bankrupt. At eighteen he was too old, because too expensive, to find another apprenticeship. So now he has been looking for a job for five months. She is afraid he will 'get into trouble' because he has nothing to do. And she notices with exasperation that he does not seem as if he *wants* a job – he is becoming unemployable.

The other nods, understanding. She is more fortunate, since her son Jimmy is working, and can swell the family income. He too is eighteen, and was unemployed for one year after leaving school because he couldn't get an apprenticeship – 'and you need a trade these days'. In fact Jimmy did not want a trade – he wanted to go to art college. Once his painting was exhibited at the Civic Centre and was admired by Princess Alexandra. But to do Art O-level? . . . his headmaster said there was no openings in art, and his parents agreed. Now Jimmy works in a timber yard as a labourer – and brings home £14 a week.

The women are resilient and passive. On their own patch they are confident: they run that advice centre, and will readily ring up the council to reassure an old lady that her house will not be pulled down next week. The last generation were confident together, but frightened in the face of officials and bosses. These women know what rights they have *not* been given, when it comes to resisting the inevitability of that drift from art school dream to the unskilled job, they are defeated. All that Geordie toughness, all the pride of generations dwindles in 1974 to the same old shrugging acceptance: 'You have to take what you can get.'

For those women, and even more for their sons, the experience is not, after all, very different. When the welfare state grants rights it does not award dignity. Not to go barefoot, not to starve, not to walk without shelter – that has been given to many who might so have suffered forty years ago. But the right also to take responsibility, to have choice; the right, not to the charity of compassion, but the dignity of respect and power . . . For that they are still waiting.

3 THE NEW TOWN

The lunch (roast turkey and trimmings) was good. The industrialists lean back, and the Reverend David Wood, Warden of Killingworth Township, stands to give his sober talk. He speaks of 'kids put out at night like dogs . . . a real fear of vandalism . . . loneliness . . . The urgency in England today is to be sure people preserve their freedom.' The men who own the factories which give jobs to the new town look interested, if uninvolved. Finally the vicar reminds them: 'The Son of God came to this earth and there was no home for him . . .'

At Killingworth there *are* homes. Killingworth – a new 'township' just north of Newcastle – was created like this earth to bring form from chaos. It was to be the solution of inner-city ills of unemployment and housing. It was to be the perfect plan: a medieval, feudal concept of a central 'castle' – called the Citadel – surrounded by areas in which the people work and live. There would be play facilities, leisure amenities, an artificial lake, and high walkways from tower block to tower block to the town centre – the feet of the people need never touch the ground. A dream city-in-miniature for the Newcastle 'overspill', Killingworth was to be apotheosis of all political architectural and social plans – a town with a 'heart'.

When you drive to Killingworth, passing through the gently affluent suburb of Gosforth, cutting across fields, seeing the farming hills of Northumberland in the distance, it comes as a sudden future-shock. It looms: grey tower-blocks, a jagged multi-story car park, a sculptured, grey concrete central building, against grey clouds. The bus conductors call it Alcatraz. In fact the description is unfair. When Killingworth was started in 1963, it did not have the benefit of a New Town Development Corporation, with all its government money. It was to be a 'township', not a heavily subsidised 'town' – and (perhaps in defiance of the more fortunate new towns proper like Washington and Cramlington) Northumberland County Council planned a show-piece. Its architecture won awards; five thousand jobs were provided in the clean new factories which surrounded it; seven and a half thousand of the planned twenty thousand people have moved in. That medieval fantasy-plan was exciting; the houses and flats – all high density – looked better than most.

Mrs Bennison thought so. She moved to Killingworth from Benwell in Newcastle – because her husband wanted to, because she liked the idea of a house no one had lived in before, because it seemed a step up from that slum. In Benwell she had been able to walk with her six children to see her mother, sisters, aunts. The shops were cheap and near, the people friendly, the old houses large, if scruffy. Shown her modern, flat-roofed, grey concrete house on three floors in Killingworth, she asked to see the fourth bedroom. It is the little one on the ground floor, they told her, which we call the 'granny room'. She doesn't smile: 'All I can say is, whoever designed that must have hated his granny!'

After about four weeks this pleasant woman of forty began to get depressed – for the first time in her life. Mrs Bennison would walk to one end of her sitting-room and look out on the grey wall of the house next door. Then she would wander across the fitted carpet to the other end and see another grey wall. 'I used to think I was the only person in the world. Funny – in these houses so close together, with all these people – to feel that. But I did.'

The change in life-style for many Killingworth people is enormous. They have not just been uprooted, but crammed into an alien shape, into a strange environment in which they are exposed. It should be a 'step up', they feel, it should be better – and so should they. It is significant that though people have lived in the town for almost ten years, the working men's club – that centre of northern working-class life – opened only last year. It is said that the council were opposed to the idea, like some of the 'private' residents. It might . . . lower the tone.

With the change come the strains. Of course many people are happy with their new homes and jobs. But there are families who come to the town contented enough, then somehow, exposed to each other as they are exposed to the bitter winds on those concrete walkways, what they see is unsatisfactory, nagging, ugly, violent. So the families split up – as Diane Spencer's did. Then, for that new-town phenomenon, the single-parent family, comes hardship amidst affluence. The rents are high: so out of an income of £19.70 social security for Diane and her two children, the rent of £6.45 makes a huge hole. Then there is that super-modern gas central heating, which seemed so posh at first. It costs far more than the coal she was used to: over £2 a week. When all the bills are paid she is left with £4.35 for food – and anxiously pushes forward scribbles on a scrap of paper to prove that it is all accounted for, every single penny. Now Christmas has been and gone she is 'up to here' in debt: 'I can't help it, because I have to give the kids a good Christmas. Could you have ready cash left out of that money? I get everything on credit.'

When the Killingworth health visitors go to welcome a new resident they meet other visitors on the doorstep: the men selling patterned nylon wall-to-wall carpets, sets of books to line the walls, new 'afrormosia' dining suites and vinyl chairs on easy terms. In one of the sparkling new Formica kitchens in the Towers – the massive blocks linked by overhead walkways, serviced by grey, coffin-shaped lifts – two women talk about life in the township. They do not consider themselves 'working class' any more; the only working-class families are the 'problem families' on the 'deck' above.

The vicar of Killingworth (or Warden, as he is called) refers to 'materialism', though it is doubtful whether those industrialists he lectures would see much wrong with it. After all, it

86

is our ethos: to make good, to do better, to get on, to improve. The health visitors talk about the web of ambition and debt which leads to 'tranquillizers being handed out at the Health Centre like Smarties'. You have to pay for your dreams. In the Citadel the handful of small shops (most are unlet because the rents are so high) pale beside the great super-store Woolco. There a notice on every counter invites you to 'CHARGE IT', to use their credit system or your Access card to buy the cassette recorders, novelty lamps, fake fur coats, telephone tables, that spill off close-packed shelves into your wire trolley. It is impossible to buy something as simple as a pencil case; you must pay twice as much for one packaged in plastic with a pink ruler. Mince in Woolco costs 48p; in Benwell back in the city you can get it for 35p. And there is no choice. Back in the city mums push their prams along the bright, busy sprawling Shields Road and gaze at a hundred different shop windows and cut-price stores, stop, chat, go to a coffee bar. Those mums do not particularly want new furniture – their material aspirations are low.

But when they are moved to an artificial community, put in houses and jobs that are a planner's dream, and seemed their own, they are carried away by fantasy. They look for something to fill the long day, when the bus service to Newcastle and the relatives is so bad – and there is Woolco. There, with no distractions, the dissatisfactions start. We build the structures; the people are lost in an alien labyrinth. And then at last reality sets in – one windy evening, as the grey clouds scud around the battlements of that citadel, and a thousand lights from a thousand little square windows shine the same, and the bills lie unpaid on that afrormosia dining table. One evening last summer a woman threw herself down to the concrete below.

Of course, the height is another problem. Last summer Mr Freeson admitted in the House of Commons that it is not good for families with young children to live in high-rise blocks. The Department of the Environment has been researching the problem for twelve years. But in high-rise blocks all over England children have been growing up for twelve years. Mr and Mrs Thompson, at 126 Bamburgh Tower, know what this means, and have asked to be moved. But once in the Towers

87

you are almost a prisoner – though the local authority, realizing its mistake, is trying gradually to move the families out. There on the top floor Mrs Thompson takes pills and Mr Thompson longs to escape to work – away from the cramped, noisy flat, where the two children rampage with nowhere else to play. Down below there is a concrete playground, but they cannot stay there all day. Outside on the 'deck' the sickening drop through the railings precludes freedom. They told Mrs Thompson at the Housing Department that if she came back with a third child in her arms she might have a chance of getting out. So they stay: worrying about their frustrated children, fighting with each other, listening through the thin grey walls to the neighbours' talk, quarrelling, making love. The lack of privacy is the final insult: 'You can't be a person here. I feel like a dog in a dog kennel, not a person.'

In Killingworth you most notice the kids: pale swathed bundles pushed by anxious windblown mums; or teenagers in baggy trousers, puffing 'tabs', waiting for a chance to whip out the spray can and give the graffiti-remover-man from the council another day's work. There are too many young people in the artificial young town. Youth-worker James Wood says that many of them are neglected by parents who both work long hours for the extra money for those bills, who give them plenty of expensive toys, but do not care what they do. Were they like that before, or did Killingworth make them that way? With jobs and houses, and money – what more do they want? In the face of some of these problems and questions those social workers and planners and politicians are likely, quietly, to withdraw: good liberals offended because their case histories bite their hand; good Tories contemptuous because the working class, with so many aspirations answered for it, cannot cope. If you have 'things' and money and a certain new status you should be happy. If not you are weak.

But they do not *ask*. At Killingworth the people have been 'given' a lot: Communicare, for example. This is a complex of health, pastoral, youth and sports centres, and a good library. It is a fine idea, and well-used. But who is it for? Those who know Killingworth well know that the families who most need help are daunted by the glossy facilities. There are kids who would never dare to ask their parents for a £2.75 family membership for the sports centre or £1.75 (plus extra each time you go) single. To be a member of the youth centre you have to pay, and to carry an identity card with a photograph. Things have been done for the people. But for many the wrong things, the planned things, the middle-class things.

At the 'other' youth club, a scruffy, blaring disco run by James Wood, the lads, forced to leave their weapons at the door, boast about their gang fights. They are the Killy Agro Boys, beneath them the Junior KAB, and beneath them the Infant KAB. Growing up in this England of concrete, the England they have been given, they use the hierarchies and the territories to construct their own fantasies. It is Clockwork Killingworth – and Burgess's Alex would know their language well. One boy, called 'Hammy' by his friends, tells how he was one of the first to come to Killingworth, seven years ago when he was eight. He missed Byker, where they'd lived with his gran, but loved the fields and trees for blackberrying and birdwatching. Dad came to the new town for a job and a house; and other people came; and more buildings went up; so that subways and walkways replaced the fields and paths. Now he waits with the KAB to pick a fight with the lads from Longbenton. He hates it. He would *like*, he says, to get a job on a farm one day, or as a forestry worker, and maybe have his own farm. But what does he *expect*? That, my little droogies, is different.

I spent much time in the North-East researching this series, which originated in my conviction that editors care little about what goes on north of Watford, unless the story is sensational. The North-East, then as now, was a forgotten outpost. It would have taken little power of clairvoyance, at the end of 1974, to predict that things would not change much, that the economic decline would continue. Ten years on, the Squire in 'Fenfield' is the same, agricultural workers are still near the bottom of the heap, and I shall still forbear to name the actual village as it would be unfair to an unchanged small community. At Killingworth the Reverend David Wood is still coping with particular problems of disillusionment and loneliness which stem from an unusually high proportion of single-parent families, and (of course) unemployment. In the high-rise 'Towers' the rate is a staggering eighty three per cent. In inner-city Newcastle much of the old housing has gone; Noble Street was finally demolished, but such hideous areas of derelict land were caught in the Heseltine housing 'moratorium', making the environment worse. The 1981 census showed the unemployment rate for Benwell as 19.5 per cent, compared with the 14.5 per cent for Newcastle as a whole – itself well above the national average. Vickers decimated its workforce after 1974 . . . and so on. This could turn into another essay; the point is that reporters rarely have the chance to retrace their steps, but it is a salutary exercise, even if only to obliterate any residual faith in political will – especially in the Britain of the Eighties.

Women

Has a Woman the Right to Fight?

(*The Times 1981*)

It is not for me to question the competence of a learned judge, and doubtless judicial compassion of a sort was exercised last week at York Crown Court. Never an advocate of vengeance, I have no wish to add to the burden of overcrowded prisons simply so that justice might be seen to be done. But justice is about values, and legal judgements are double-edged: they reflect society's attitudes as well as affect them. That is why women will consider a 'sentence' passed last week at York an affront, even an insult, to their sex. It is why I do doubt, not the competence of Judge Stanley Price, but his wisdom; certainly I question the correctness of his decision.

The case was scarcely reported; this is what happened. A few months ago, Diana Lee, who is nineteen years old, missed the last bus to her home near Scarborough, after seeing that her pony was secure in its field two miles away. Though it was dark and late she started to walk. Melvyn Maguire, a 'handyman' aged twenty-four, was taking a lift home with a friend when he saw the girl walking along the lane. Dropped off at his house, Maguire ran back over a mile, confronted her, pretended to be a policeman, pounced on her from behind, dragged her into a lonely field, attacked her, knelt upon her, and told her that he was going to kill her.

In such a situation, most people, let alone a young woman, would be helpless with shock and fear. Terrified, believing she was about to be murdered (and sexual assault, too, cannot have been far from her mind) Miss Lee nevertheless managed to pull out the small sheath knife she kept for cutting the string on her pony's bales of hay, and stuck it in Maguire's neck. Because of her courage and presence of mind, and because she was fortunate to be carrying the means to defend herself, her assailant walks free today. Though a jury unanimously found him guilty of threatening to kill her, the judge showed apparent sympathy to the man, telling him: 'This young lady inflicted a very considerable punishment on you.' Maguire was given a twelve-month suspended sentence and walked out, smiling.

While I have never studied jurisprudence, nor even sat long hours in the press boxes at the Old Bailey, studying the mysteries of the law, it seems obvious that something is grievously wrong. Diana Lee did not coolly decide (lying there upon the ground) that this premeditated assault was an affront to her dignity and therefore merited 'punishment'. She was struggling to defend herself against a vicious attack which she believed might lead to her death. Everyone is entitled to use a reasonable amount of self-defence against aggression; for a judge to call the result of the self-defence a 'punishment' seems to fling judicial wisdom out of the window.

What if Diana Lee had been an elderly man who was attacked by a mugger but managed to jab his assailant in the eye with his walking-stick? Would the fact that the thug had to be treated at the local eye hospital somehow cancel out the brutality of the attack? Or what if Miss Lee had been a twelve-year-old girl, dragged into that lonely field with a view to some disgusting assault. If she had picked up a hefty stone and bashed the man on the head, causing momentary concussion and subsequent fits of dizziness, would we then nod sagely with a judge who remarked that the attacker had been punished enough? We would not. There is no doubt that in such cases a judge would view a poke in the eye or a blow on the head as irrelevant to the fact that an unprovoked attack had taken place on an innocent person, that the attack was a dreadful and traumatic experience, that the victim's courage had prevented a far worse crime – and that in order to protect the public the court should impose an appropriate punishment.

The case raises two significant points – the first about the values enshrined within our sentencing structure, and the second about the attitude of the judiciary towards women. In the first place: does it not seem absurd that we appear to view crimes against property with more gravity than crimes against the person? When our inner cities are riot-torn, the sounds of shattering plate glass and the sight of discriminate looting give way to cries of outrage, and calls for fines, for short sharp shocks, for stiff sentences. Our prisons are full of women and men doing time for petty theft. Property rules – OK. That there should be a radical reassessment of priorities must be obvious to anyone who believes that a theory of justice involves the identification of values which the legal system then seeks to realize. Diana Lee must derive scant comfort from the sense that a judge might have been more indignant had she been a music-centre in a looted hi-fi shop window.

Second: that the law is often unfair to women in rape cases should be clear to anyone who has studied the evidence. For the past twelve years or so the Women's Movement (with the trade union movement the most significant social development of this century) has set up rape crisis centres and attempted to help battered wives, and pointed an accusing finger at the police and courts for frequently assuming that women somehow ask, and therefore deserve, to be victims of violence.

Of course, these questioners of society's received 'values' have been ridiculed. On my desk is a new book, called *No Turning Point* (published by The Women's Press), which raises the question of women and violence in the kind of language that is easy to ridicule. It says: 'Individual acts of terrorism (in the home and street) become expressions of collective control through the operation of the state. The support the male receives from the state transforms the individual use of force and its threat into social power.' Translate that into plain English and its relevance to Diana Lee's case is clear – showing that the injustice transcends the fact that one man should have been imprisoned, to teach him a lesson and to protect other women. Maguire's attack on Diana Lee is made legitimate because the judge let him off, and that means that more men will think women walking alone are fair game. As evidence of the kind of abuse men lay upon women, Germaine Greer, in *The Female Eunuch*, cited a judge who in 1969 called a girl who had been raped a 'flibbertigibbet'. Today we seem to think the streets are so safe for women that we bring prosecutions against those mistrustful females who seek to protect themselves (as in a recent case) by carrying 'offensive weapons' like incapacitating sprays. Now we have the Maguire case, in which a judge has allowed a man guilty of an appalling attack upon a girl to go free *because* his victim protected herself.

It may not have been in that particular judge's mind, but it is hard to avoid the conclusion (studying so many cases of rape and assault) that the collective judicial wisdom says that a woman has no *right* to walk alone at night, and no right to fight back against attack. No right, in fact, to that real compassion and protection of the law that would have been given to Diana Lee's pony, had some passing thug thrown the poor creature to the ground, and most cruelly threatened its life.

Women marched into Soho around this time carrying banners which proclaimed, 'Women reclaim the night'. I had spent the Seventies supporting penal reform, and writing articles about it for the *New Statesman*; it was curious to find myself on the other side of the fence. Indeed honesty compels me to point out that here I echo the very words I quoted (disapprovingly) in the profile of Margaret Thatcher: 'In our desire for humanitarian reform we have lost sight of the purpose of the courts and the true aim of punishment.' The start of the Eighties saw a shift in liberal attitude on two fronts, censorship and punishment, both influenced by the Women's Movement. Weighing up two freedoms: the freedom to publish etc, and the freedom thereby to show women exploited, humiliated, even 'snuffed', many women questioned the former. And feminists who might once have advocated leniency in the courts heard one too many judge rebuke a woman for being out late at night and 'inviting' attack. Incidentally, none of this is new. In 1912 Rebecca West wrote: 'The social liberty of a respectable woman is circumscribed by the vices of men. A woman who wishes to go about London alone by night, or to look at the shop windows in Bond Street in the afternoon, encounters unpleasantness due to the accidents of the man-made social system. There is even an idea that women should regulate their dress according to men's lack of self-control rather than their own comfort.'

Not the Gentle Sex

(*The Times 1981*)

Last week justice caught up at last with more Nazi thugs, reminding us yet again that the old excuse of 'obeying orders' does not excuse a single human being from responsibility for his or her own actions – not at the Bastille, nor at Mi Lai, nor at Majdanek. Apart from provoking the thought that it might be a good idea to make the wearing of the swastika (sported proudly now by our home-bred thugs) illegal as an offence against public order and decency, the trial in Dusseldorf carried a significant lesson for women. Once Hermine Ryan and Hildegard Lachert were little girls, probably rocking flaxen-haired dolls in their little arms and crooning '*Guten Abend, gute Nacht* . . .' They grew up, donned uniforms and power and became monsters their victims nicknamed the Mare and Bloody Brigitta, relishing the sensation of toe-cap against bone and the sound of human screams. There, in the obscenity of Majdanek, they proved their equality: an equality of evil.

If I say that the crimes and the punishment of those two women are a blow for the Women's Movement, do not think me cynical, nor that I am equating our demand for equality and respect with the bestiality of two warped women. No; the point is, there is a powerful little myth that needs, urgently and finally, to be laid to rest – and Ryan and Lachert have stamped grimly upon its grave. We are not the gentle sex, nor have we ever been; and it is a grave disservice to mankind to assume that half of it has the monopoly on gentleness and compassion. Of course, most men like to think of women as gentle, intuitive, swayed by pleasant emotions. It fixes us for ever in a certain useful and admirable role – smoothing pillows, addressing our minds to babies' bottoms, and being there at night with the slippers warming, the casserole bubbling, and the tender inquiry, 'How was your day, dear?' I am not mocking that picture, because there is nothing laughable about people ministering to each other out of love; and if one ministers more than the other and both are happy, so be it. The trouble is, though ministering may be a woman's private choice, it comes to be a sort of general requirement for the sex. And still many men think complacently with Keats,

> God! She is a milk-white lamb that bleats
> For man's protection.

God! and our crimes are crimes of passion or of hormone, as we scamper after our emotions like pussy-cats after china bowls of cream, with clichés tied around our necks.

It is a myth that women bolster. A few weeks ago I did a television interview with a representative of the '300 Group', which aims to get more women into Parliament, and instil even more with the confidence to think that one day they might. One thing Lesley Abdela implied has been bothering me ever since: that if more women become MPs they will be, somehow, *different*: better, more understanding, more caring. Now that is just another way of perpetrating the old 'saints and angels' stereotype that bleats, if not for man's protection, for his admiration. Cyril Connolly expressed what is the delusion of many women as well as most men: 'When every unkind word about women has been said, we still have to admit . . . that they are nicer than men. They are more devoted, more unselfish, and more emotionally sincere.'

Much as I would like that to be true, the suspicion that it is nonsense nags like a sore truth. I am as committed as any sensible woman to the cause of equality, but surely we must start by being scrupulously honest and rigorously logical about who we are and what we want. Yes, let us see more women in Parliament, in industry, in the trade union hierarchy, and in the chair at British Rail as well as at many committees. But this vision of gentle people passing gentle laws, and never shouting each other down, and feeling (for women feel these things) pity for the poor and compassion for the single mother and indignation on behalf of the oppressed in the Third World (show a woman a picture of a starving child and tears will fill her eyes) . . . this vision of a female utopia *bleats* once more. The land of the Houyhnhnms was not ruled by mares. In any case, remember the Mare.

There is no evidence that can lead to the conclusion (attractive though it might be) that women in authority exhibit those miraculous and virtuous qualities that are traditionally supposed to be feminine, nor that they identify with issues other women care about. There is no reason to suppose that a deeply conservative woman MP is more likely to be sympathetic to questions about abortion, divorce or child benefit than a liberal male; no reason to think that Nancy Reagan will be more concerned about the situation of poor black women in the deep South than the maintenance of America's full defence capability. Horrified world attention fixed upon Frau Ryan and Frau Lachert because they are women, and women are not supposed to behave like that. But *people* are not supposed to behave like that, and the most ardent feminist cannot suppose that had the SS and SA been run by women the Nazi atrocities would not have taken place.

The worst abuse committed feminists pour upon the Prime Minister is that she is the living embodiment of the male-substitute theory; they accuse her of being just like a man. It begs the question of what it means to be like a man or like a woman. If Roy Hattersley suddenly shows how deeply and emotionally he feels about the Labour Party, is he accused of being womanish? It is remarkably unfair of women who want other women to reach positions of power and influence to turn round and accuse Mrs Thatcher of being like a man when she exhibits the sort of toughness that power demands. Mrs Thatcher is as hard-headed as Denis Healey and as wily as

Harold Wilson – because she is a politician. She is as tough as even Peter Shore or Ian Gilmour would have to be were they (singly, not together) to inhabit Downing Street. Though the Prime Minister's particular brand of inflexibility may be her own private way of scotching the 'little-woman-who-changes-her-mind' myth, her sex is no more relevant to her policies than it was when she was elected.

So if, as I am saying, the only thing that matters in politics is what a person is like, not what sex, why do I still thump my tub and say that more women should whinny instead of bleat and get themselves into positions of power? It is not because I think they will be better at it, nor because I think they could force a return to the compassionate society – or anything so fanciful. It is simply because it is essential to the health of a democracy to have the greatest possible number of its people interested in politics – able to vote with knowledge and gusto, to give their MP informed criticism, to identify important issues, and to see politics as what it is: not a power game played out by a handful of men in one building, but the organization of the polity, the whole people.

Traditionally the average women is bored by all that – and small wonder, when you consider the braying insults that emanate from the Mother of Parliaments, the intellectual ineptitude of half the Tory back benches, and the dead *polit-bureau* rhetoric that entombs empathy at Labour Party conferences. Up until now politics has been conducted by men for men; the more women heave themselves into positions of power, and are *seen* to be achieving, the less that will be so. People are imitative. Just as we need black policemen and a black middle class to give young West Indians a new self-image, so we need more women to represent the people, to show other women that their equality is as unquestionable as their numbers. But we don't need myths, or special pleading. If you accept that women are as capable as men of building a heaven (if there is one to be built), you must not be surprised if we also demonstrate ruthlessness, corruption, and cunning – or even the hellish subhumanity of a concentration camp guard.

This was written before the phenomenon of a specifically female involvement with the peace movement was noticed by our bemused news editors. The subject became one (see page 118) that aroused an enormous response from readers.

After this piece was published a well-known male writer approached me at the annual *Spectator* summer party and cried out, with great passion, that if what I said about women was true he no longer wanted to live. To the best of my knowledge he is still writing.

Ecce Puella

(*The Times* 1982)

There is an eighteenth-century print which shows two mid-wives bursting into the elegant drawing-room where a father-to-be is waiting. 'C'est un fils, Monsieur!' is the happy title, and Monsieur is throwing up his arms with joy – which is a little strange since the babe displayed cannot be less than three months old. The son and heir: Ecce Puer. This litany continues in maternity wards up and down the land – a boy, they say, ensuring continuity. Most families can indulge their patrilineal longings in private; land and title complicate the issue; but when we are forced to consider the succession to the British throne we find ourselves, not surprisingly, knee-deep in atavistic prejudice.

Certainly that is the view of the Member for Nottingham West. Michael English is proposing a Private Member's Bill which will seek to bring our law of succession into line with that of Sweden, where, since 1979, the right of accession to the throne has passed to the eldest child, irrespective of sex. Strictly speaking the term primogeniture should imply just that: the right of the first-born, just as ultimogeniture used sometimes to favour the youngest child. But in practice this

103

system of inheritance gave land and title to the primogeni*tus* – the first-born *male*. Needless to say, Michael English is not unaware of a certain impending happy event. He has timed his onslaught to coincide with the pregnancy of the Princess of Wales, saying that he believes in equality of the sexes and that, despite the many equalities that exist, this one is the hardest to change. Ensure the right of Prince Charles's first-born to the throne whatever its sex, and we will create a better climate to which to further the general cause of women.

Why *should* it be the hardest to change? Surely, if the Princess of Wales were to produce three or four daughters, all as charming as herself, few publicly would bewail the lack of a son? But the old common law of primogeniture is not about personalities. It throbs deep in the feudal memory of the nation – when decreeing that lands and titles must pass to the eldest son simplified matters, prevented the great estates from being broken up, and ensured that kings knew whom they were dealing with.

Political expediency, then – but more. The assumption of Demosthenes ('One thing is admitted, that males and the issue of males have the first title to inheritances . . .') is echoed in the *Leges Saxonum*: 'On the death of the father or mother the inheritance goes to the son, not the daughter . . .'. Under Salic Law no woman could ever inherit (which is why the crowns of Great Britain and Hanover became separated when Victoria became Queen). By the late Middle Ages we sense a need to justify: 'Because women lose the name of their ancestor, and by marriage usually are transferred to another family, they participate seldom in heirship with males'. It is left to John Knox to put it plainly: 'The holy ghost doth manifestly say: I suffer not that women usurp authority over men.'

Yet though the monstrous regiment of misogynists have much to say on the matter, I turn to feminist authorities (de Beauvoir, Greer, Rowbottom, *et al*) in vain. They would probably argue that the issue is peripheral: that we should do better to agitate for the abolition of the monarchy than for an extension of the rights of princesses. Perhaps – but then we should miss a good opportunity for reform by stealth and example. Michael English has, enterprisingly, disinterred one issue which *both* those concerned with women's rights and those who are interested in the preservation of the monarchy should take seriously.

Both arguments hinge upon symbolism – that which the republican may dislike, but which he/she cannot deny. To take first the feminist issue of simple equality: how can we, as a nation, think it enough to write equality within the statute book, yet ignore that symbolic inequality at the heart of our ceremonial? Is it possible – with the magnificent reign of Victoria still in living memory, with Elizabeth II upon the throne and with a popular young Princess of Wales expecting a baby — that we can still acquiesce in the nonsense that would set that baby aside in favour of a subsequent child, if she is a girl and he a boy? Imagine if Prince Charles were to have three daughters, then, after a long gap, a son. Is it just that the eldest girl should be brought up as heir to the throne, only to be told one day, 'C'est un fils – this is what we have been waiting for – sorry, Your Royal Highness, you just won't do'? Michael English argues that to change this would reverberate right through our institutions and attitudes – and I think he is right. As for the die-hard patriots – well, I suspect that with one woman reigning and another ruling, with Shirley Williams watching, and with the terrible possibility that (courtesy of Mr English) the Princess of Wales might produce a primogenita, a little epidemic of that common disease (known specially to affect older men) called gynaecocrataphobia could sweep the clubs. These who fear the rule of women yet love the monarchy should reconsider their prejudice.

Why give ammunition to those who say that the institution is out of date? We have seen thrones topple; we have witnessed the rise of monocracy – with Hitler, Mussolini, Stalin, Franco, Nasser, Sukarno as just a few shining examples; the Presidency was diminished for ever after Watergate. Republicans may be right to call our monarchy anachronistic; what matters is that most people would prefer it to any other system. Yet the health of the monarchy can be judged by its ability to shift imperceptibly with the time – the 'walkabout' symbolically as necessary as the golden coach.

It would suit the republican's purpose well were British conservatism to defeat Mr English's Bill. Then the finger of derision could indeed be pointed at the Palace and the tumbril wheels well oiled – no more proof needed that the institution has outlived itself. It is an interesting thought – feminists (pink) joining force with monarchists (blue) to demand the commonsensical equal rights for the Queen's grandchildren that we should all expect for our own.

Mercifully (or should I say, unfortunately?) the Establishment did not have to cross this particular Rubicon. On 21 June 1982 Prince William Arthur Philip Louis was born.

Why the PM Gets Away With It

(*Sunday Times 1983*)

When President Reagan called the Prime Minister the 'best man in England', we have to assume he was being complimentary, although there are some of us who would grimace at the backhandedness (or cackhandedness) of the phrase. Yet, when the Iron Lady landed on the Falklands, her sovereign territory, bowed her head by graves but reached the stratosphere with her flights of rhetoric, we have surely witnessed the apotheosis of Margaret Thatcher. Now, courtesy of Ronald Reagan, she rises through the rosy MGM sunset into a Valhalla peopled by strong male gods.

Images nudge each other in my mind. One is of Mrs Thatcher, woman as victor, squinting down the sights of a 105mm weapon, and firing the shell at the barren strip called Pleasant Island. The other is of the camp at Greenham Common, women as peacemakers, women who expressly exclude men from their action because, they say, it is men who are violent, who love war and victory, and resort too quickly to roughness. Yet it is not only feminists who think that. On the contrary, it is the most conservative and conventional view, and one that President Reagan implicitly shares. It says that one sex has the monopoly on compassion, gentleness, kindness; the other is benighted *en masse* by aggressive and *macho* values.

I have said it before, and will no doubt repeat myself, that the myth is a dangerous delusion. That sort of patronage fixes women for ever in the role of nurse and mother, smoothing brows and understanding all. Peace. People. Emotions. Etc. What astonishes me is that so many feminists bolster the myth – paying lipservice to equality, but in fact moving further towards a divine assumption that women are more than equal, they are morally and spiritually superior.

Here I must make two things crystal clear. First, I would take it amiss to be called the best man at the *Sunday Times* because I like being a woman and tend to prefer the company of women to that of men. Second, I wholly endorse and approve the conviction that leads the women at Greenham to continue their protest in the cold and dark whilst you and I are snug at home. But to base such a protest on the premise that women are more peace-loving and gentle than men, to weave baby clothes in the railings and exalt a sort of folksy femininity as a universal verity – that seems to me to pander to the old myth/prejudice that keeps women in their place. It does injury not only to equality, but to truth.

Mrs Thatcher has been called by Denis Healey a 'bargain-basement Boadicea', and must welcome any comparison with the warrior-queen who, in the space of two months, slaughtered more Romans and destroyed more of their property than did Caractacus in nine years of guerrilla warfare. Elizabeth I, Catherine the Great . . . names leap from history. Then what about Indira Gandhi, Golda Meir, Mrs Bandaranaike, Mrs Thatcher . . . each of them more combative and ruthless than ten Reagans rolled into one. Guerrilla camps in the Middle East are full of passionate young women prepared to do violence for their cause, and the IRA knows well that women are excellent planters of bombs. And on a domestic level, who shows the greater violence towards children, men or women? Surely there, as with the rest, is equality.

Of course there are great differences between men and women, as between people – not least, physical strength. In the ability to use force women are hampered. But in the capacity, or *will* to use force – is there such a great difference? When the action does not depend upon muscle . . . because the victims are weak, or because the means is a bomb or weapon, or perhaps because the woman in question is head of a war cabinet which simply has to say the word to sink an enemy ship outside a total exclusion zone . . . what then?

When Mrs Thatcher shot her Falklands gun she wasn't merely posing; it was genuine fantasy, as real as her Churchillian rhetoric, ('They died that others might gain their freedom, etc.'). But how does she get away with it? Can you imagine Heseltine, Foot or Healey carrying it off with such heart-clutching, mind-boggling, stomach-churning panache? No. And why? The secret, President Reagan, is in the sex. The PM gets away with it, not because she is 'the best man in England', but because she is a woman. Women are not expected to be as tough as men. When they are, they gain additional kudos in this myth-ridden society for being what no one expects them to be. Male leaders have but one narrow role to play. Mrs Thatcher can be Boadicea, Victoria, Churchillia, mother, Forces pin-up, and bereaved war widow at once. With, of course, a touch of the Modesty Blaise.

Let us return from the Falklands to that other bleak place, Greenham Common, and a suggestion that neither side will welcome: that Mrs Thatcher and the Greenham women have much in common, except aims. The one exploits her sex quite brilliantly, the others knew, with great astuteness, that it was the 'women-only' aspect of their actions that would get the attention. Both use rampant sentiment (the graves, the baby clothes) to achieve ends that are pretty hard-headed.

The Greenham women are tough and (be sure of it) will not be moved. Mrs Thatcher is tough and (we know) will not be moved — and such assertiveness is what women are trained *not* to show. Both sides want power; both sides are willing to take positive action towards that end. You see, we must untie the pussy-cat bows of simple cliché from our necks. Mrs Thatcher is, for better, for worse, President Reagan, a woman – with all the deviousness, toughness, vanity, aggression, ambition, ruthlessness and guts that that implies.

Let Rebecca West enter the fray. Her review (in the *Daily News*, 13 April 1917) of a book called *War, Peace and the Future* by an unfortunate Miss Ellen Key, is devastating – and relevant:

> Miss Key's feminism has always been peculiar. It has not been a form of the worship of life, it has not been an aspiration that women should contribute more largely to the development of humanity by the exercise of intelligence and genius; it has been woman-worship. Women need not trouble to develop any human qualities. They are merely to sit still and be as female as they can, taking as their ideal not the untiring St Teresa, but the Sacred Cow of the Universe. There is a magic about mere femaleness which will enable them so to regenerate the world. And now mere femaleness is going to end the war. It appears that men have failed to notice that the war is unpleasant. This news is going to be broken to them by women, and then there will be eternal peace.

West admitted, 'it is probable that the emotional driving force of a peace movement will come from women', but asserted, 'this is not to be used as an argument for woman-worship.' There is no reason not to suppose that this argument will go on and on.

The Mysterious Greenham Phenomenon

(*Sunday Times 1983*)

'Have you read *Three Guineas?*' the woman asked. 'Oh, you should read it. Very interesting, very relevant to us.' Immediately, amidst the orange tents, plastic margarine tubs and smoking fires of Greenham Common, another spirit was invoked: that of the Bloomsbury Sybil, the waspish mind and anguished spirit who prefigured, in bookish drawing rooms, the Berkshire battle.

It was salutary to be pointed in that useful direction by a well-knitted mind, divested (on this cold sunny day) of the fabled woolly hat. In her treatise on women and war (published in 1938) Virginia Woolf noted: 'The number of societies run directly or indirectly by Englishwomen in the cause of peace is too long to quote.' Last weekend's demonstration proved that women are, once again, a most potent force in a new peace movement. There is an increasing amount of literature which asserts, directly or obliquely, what Mrs Woolf suggested forty-five years ago: that there is a fundamental, though unproven, difference between *most* women and *most* (not all) men, for whom war is a profession. Considering human rage and helplessness on regarding savage photographs of war, Woolf says this:

> That emotion, that very positive emotion demands something more positive than a name written on a sheet of paper . . . some more energetic, some more active method of expressing our belief that war is inhuman, that war is, as Wilfred Owen put it, insupportable horrible and beastly, seems to be required. But rhetoric apart, what more active method is open to us?

That 'us' meant 'women', and there is no doubt that Leslie Stephen's daughter approved of what is now called 'direct action'.

> Certainly the one great political achievement of the educated man's daughter cost her over half a century of the most exhausting and menial labour; kept her trudging in processions . . . speaking on street corners; finally, because she used force, sent her to prison . . .

Today, Mrs Woolf would be pilloried in the *Daily Mail* for her rejection of patriotism. She says women should see themselves as outside its rhetoric: 'For, the outsider will say, in fact as a woman I have no country. As a woman I want no country. As a woman my country is the whole world.'

That alternative rhetoric is familiar. Return to Greenham Common, view the wool webs, the *papier-mâché* masks, the eccentric respelling of words like 'wimmin', the improbable cosiness of the little tents in a landscape of wire fencing and policemen – and what *is* it that is there? All those women in early peace campaigns would have recognized the phenomenon.

It is more than a stand against cruise missiles. It is an assertion (the women say) of compassionate and emotional feminine values set against the male world of mechanistic logic and aggression. In the *Antigone* the doomed, recalcitrant

112

heroine says, 'It is not my nature to join in hating, but in loving.' To which the ruler Creon replies, 'Pass, then, to the world of the dead, and if thou must needs love, love them. While I live no woman shall rule me.'

Now, a jump-cut. The scene is the conference centre at Westminster Cathedral, a stone's throw from the House of Commons, where a new, counter-movement is being launched. Women cram the small room, in tens not thousands; the table-cloth is blue. Lady Olga Maitland announces the launch of 'Women For Defence', and there is more of the rhetoric of gender: 'We are aware of the anxiety of mothers, wives, grandmothers . . . we shall talk sympathetically, women to women . . . from three women in a kitchen to a group at a coffee morning . . . we desperately want peace for our families, but we call upon the women of this country to face up to the fact of a potential bullying aggressor.' So, one group of women invoke matriarchal values in the name of peace. This group of women also invokes matriarchal values but wants to keep the bomb for insurance with Michael Heseltine the Man from the Pru.

Just as the women at Greenham run the risk of overdoing the mystical-earth-mother element (and many feminists resent it – who, after all, may not *have* children), so there is no doubt that Lady Olga and her friends are jumping on a bandwagon here. Fear, they say, is sweeping the women of Britain; a 'frenzy' of fear . . . and that word recalls Maenads. The women in this room look calm and well groomed, but the astonishing fact is this: they, and Winston S. Churchill who is beaming in the front row, and indeed the whole government, are themselves frightened enough of the scruffy women at Greenham to seek to counter them by all the power of wealth, organization, and even by sombre and symbolic trips to the Berlin Wall.

The mystery deepens. For the Greenham phenomenon has passed through three stages so far. First indifference, then curiosity, then derision and fear. When the attention came it was because the camp was 'women-only' and it gave headline writers a field-day. Though perhaps motivated by mistaken prejudice, the separatism was politically astute. Yet the women, naive though it may seem, did not bargain for the vitriol. Mention, now, that you are paying a visit to Greenham and the jokes will come thick and fast: 'Are you turning into a lesbian?' 'Better take a bodyguard!' or (puzzled) 'Why do those harridans make themselves look so awful?' One male writer went so far as to suggest that, now the bitter Spring is here, they should wear 'the more feminine skirts'. As Virginia Woolf quipped, 'The cat is out of the bag, and it is a Tom.' Women should not sit around in mud, let alone climb fences, not necessarily because they are wrong, but because such action is unfeminine. All right to sign petitions and organize meetings behind blue table cloths. But to take it all so very seriously that they are willing to be uncomfortable, like soldiers . . . No, that is what attracts the fear, and subsequent hostility or derision.

Resentment against them is not only from the right. A. J. P. Taylor, one of the founders of CND, has written that the peace movement seems now to have been taken over by feminism. There are those within CND who query separatism, and fear that it will split the movement. Quite rightly, many men take offence at the notion that one sex has sewn up compassion. That said, the most perfunctory reading of anthropological texts fixes the feminist obsession with patriarchal values firmly within scholarship. In primitive cultures matriarchy was/is synonymous with freedom, equality, hospitality, caring; patriarchy with destructiveness, sadism, aggression.

In *The Anatomy of Human Destructiveness*, Erich Fromm quotes with approval the research of Bachofen, whose work of 1861 was rejected until today because of statements like this: 'An air of tender humanity, discernible even in the facial expression of Egyptian statuary, permeates the culture of the matriarchal world.' *Pace* Mrs Thatcher, Mrs Ghandi *et al*, always remembering the exceptions, most women would assert with confidence that they are 'more emotional' than men. Fromm suggests as much, though he warns '. . . there is not a simple relationship between male-ness and self-assertive aggressiveness, but a highly complex one about whose details we know nothing.' And of course all mass movements are cursed with oversimplification.

There is a complication here: the interesting point about the issue in question is that the women are *not* inclined to sit back

114

with feminine passivity musing upon Utopia. So what gives muscle to the matriarchy? Another scene; another clue. It is an Ecumenical Centre in West London, packed for a meeting about cruise missiles which the Notting Hill Labour Party has organized. Tony Benn will speak; before him Rebecca Johnson from Greenham – and she with the suffragette purple, green and white in her hair has already been to prison twice. Before she starts she confesses she is 'terrified'; when she stands she is transformed: 'I want to bring you something of the spirit of Greenham . . .' She breaks, without warning, into song. For a second you (the controlled, the dubious) feel embarrassed, then notice that the eyes of the young women around, mostly young and fashionably dressed, are moist and their gaze rapt. They *want* this message: 'It is urgent . . . you can't expect to be led, you must take personal responsibility . . .'

The speech, overlong but compelling, is delivered in front of the Christian cross which (given the nature of the place) hangs behind, and its tone suggest an answer to the mystery, for two reasons. First, because it is an expression of complete faith: the woman uses the cadences of Evangelism and the same appeal for personal commitment, the same demand that the heart should be changed from within and then the world changed too.

Speaking without a single note and no sign of terror, Rebecca Johnson invokes images – of church congregations containing a majority of women, as they always have; of female medieval mystics like Julian of Norwich; of the religious zeal of Antigone that was only in part sisterly; of women murdered as witches, or martyrs. There is a sense that a strong faith in peace has filled a spiritual gap – reaching up towards the apparent impossibility Christ preached, in language as simple.

The second important factor is the confidence. When Greenham Common women on television answer Brian Walden's request for their alternative strategy with the unblinking answer, '*love*', it is enough to make even a sympathizer wince. They would argue that the wince proves that we have become so numbed by the mystifying terminology of pre-emptive strike, SS20, and deployment, that we are shamed by the moral imperatives that transcend all that. Yet something gives these women the confidence to assert them, even in the unfriendly territory of a television studio; just as Rebecca Johnson was as assured as Tony Benn. It could be that the current activity of women for peace is not so much to do with the truth or untruth of the patriarchal argument, but with an historical coincidence. In the early Eighties we are witnessing a simultaneous growth of spiritual need and political awareness as well as sheer confidence in women who have been brought up in the light shed by the Women's Liberation Movement of the Sixties and Seventies – so that they, who might have been mere backroom organizers or passive supporters of a peace movement, are now its most active participants.

The word for the mood is ardent – and it cannot be explained away by neurosis, nor smears ('the tools of Moscow' etc), still less by patronage. Women For Defence have a mission to explain 'to the women of Britain' that the bomb is necessary, 'because they don't understand'. It might be that women understand with great clarity the central political issue of the age – one outlined presciently in *The Times* of 11 July 1936 by Lord Londonderry: 'The question we are asking ourselves is whether man is capable of enjoying the new fruits of scientific knowledge, or whether by their misuse he will bring about the destruction of himself and the edifice of civilization.'

If little revolutions endure the stages of indifference, curiosity and hosility, the fourth one is acceptance – and there are signs at Greenham that it is starting to happen. Sunny morning, police patrolling – and a sleek grey-haired man in a slick grey jacket pulls up in his car. He wants to cut hair. Cut *hair*? Yes, he is a hairdresser and he thought he might give some free trims 'as his contribution to the cause'. Then the red post van draws up, a cheerful good morning, and he delivers a bundle of letters to the women – as if this flap of tents were a housing estate, home. Women get up slowly and make breakfast, a little cagey of visitors (the hostile press hurt) but willing to explain, and to show their painted sign – a pastiche of the RAF one behind them which says welcome to the base. Behind them, the miles and miles of fencing symbolize our defence.

Against what? The depersonalized aggressor? Or these trouble-some females who have written themselves so largely into the language – one of whom sits in the open, head bowed, as the friendly local hairdresser trims, with great precision, her perfectly normal fringe.

The women at Greenham Common were *the* subject of 1982–83, albeit one that most editors disliked. They did not succeed; in November 1983 (inevitably), cruise missiles were flown into the base, and the Secretary of State for Defence admitted, in the House of Commons, that anyone who approached them might well be shot. It was then that the women seemed to gain more sympathy for their vigil; after all, the polls had shown that nearly three quarters of the great British public were against cruise. So the 'freaks' were not so freakish after all.

The story behind this article is revealing. What appears here (the original) is not quite what appeared in the *Sunday Times*. One of the most disturbing and repellent aspects of Greenham was its coverage in the press: with two exceptions the national papers refused to take the women seriously, and when finally they had to admit that they were indubitably *there*, there were jeers and smears. Suzanne Lowry was then Editor of the 'Look' pages, and suggested I write a report. I was not at all sympathetic to the separatism or the 'folksiness' and had written as much; yet after a long cold day outside those gates I was impressed by those tenacious grand-daughters of the suffragettes. I set out to write a piece that would (*fairly*) describe what I saw, and consider the involve-ment of women in the whole issue of nuclear defence; that was all. The article was so fair that the then Editor of the paper disliked it, and did not want to print the (commissioned) piece. It took Lowry two hours of spirited argument to per-suade him; she then had to agree to cuts and changes, small but telling, which would be tedious to list here. Just one example: Winston S. Churchill *was* in the front row of Lady Olga Maitland's inaugural meeting: I saw him, other repor-ters saw him, and it is reasonable to assume that he was proud to be seen . . . but my reference to him was deleted. So as far as my newspaper was concerned, he was not there.

Six months later cruise came, and Suzanne Lowry was no longer there to commission such pieces and to defend them. Still, about seventy per cent of the huge postbag we received was sympathetic to the women's stand. The readers, thank goodness, are prepared to read beyond the prejudice of the leader pages in their newspapers.

Family Life

26 November 1975

I remembered pushing, breathing through a mouth like the Sahara. Then at 5 am I regained consciousness in my small cubicle, staring confusedly at the dim red light they leave burning in the rooms of the sick, wondering what had happened. Needing a bedpan I groped stiffly for the bell, brain clearing, awareness dawning. By the time the nurse came I knew – though my hand still felt my stomach to see if he was still there. 'What happened?' I asked. She looked distressed: 'Don't you know? You had your baby and it was a little boy . . . and he isn't alive.'

For three hours, until my husband came, I could not cry. They had taken me into hospital two weeks earlier to rest because of my lack of weight; they had induced the birth three weeks early in a (now I see) desperate attempt to prevent his inevitable death inside me; the night before the labour I rang a friend and said I was convinced my baby would die. But such is the gap between what the heart hopes and the mind knows, that I could not take in the fate I had predicted. During sixteen hours of awful pain, made worse by the anxiety, I hoped he would live, I expected him to live, I laboured for his life. Now my husband and I were left to weep in each other's arms – like all parents of still-born babies devastated by the extent of the love and loss we felt for someone we had never met.

The following days taught me more about the nature of motherhood – as well as of suffering – than did the birth of my first son, Daniel, who is now two. The gap ached – so much so that one sleepless tormented night I tiptoed downstairs to get Daniel's teddy bear to take back to bed: the vacancy in the womb had been replaced by an emptiness in my arms and some small thing, anything, was necessary to fill it (and they send women to prison for stealing babies).

On the fourth day after the birth-death I awoke to find my breasts full of milk – nature's cruellest irony – ready to feed the baby who was not there. Like a full cow past milking time, I cried. And like an animal I could not understand: all the intellectual/feminist debate on the nature of motherhood and the needs of the family dissolved beside the awfulness of the physical loss, and need. For nine months I had been prepared for a baby. Without that baby I was still a mother, ready, and cheated. When I cried bitterly three nights in succession that I hated being a woman, hated being married, hated being trapped, I was expressing an awareness more fundamental than that of my role, more an unwilling acceptance of my function.

He was born and died on the Wednesday. On Friday I was discharged from the hospital – the doctors and nurses, though kind and upset, unable (I sensed) to cope. Out of place; amidst waiting pregnant women, and the mewls of the newborn, and post-natally depressed girls staring helplessly into metal cots full of responsibility, had come death, and it was an intrusion. Some mothers of still-born babies want to see and hold their dead baby, though I did not. But significantly, it was never suggested. Those who have escaped the experience cannot approach its meaning: that a still-born child is a real person to the mother (and father, in this case) who bore him/her.

One day at home a friend rang, and I heard my mother say, 'Bel lost her baby.' The euphemism outraged me. For I did not lose him like an umbrella or a lover. He was born and died. To be accurate he was born dead: the ultimate contradiction in terms, so mysterious it defies analysis. When I heard that acquaintances thought I had miscarried I was equally outraged – it seemed important that they should realize the gulf between that sad accident and what we had been through.

That gulf is symbolized most clearly by the requirements of bureaucracy: the fact that my husband had to go, one bleak rainy day, to get a piece of paper from the hospital, then go to the Registrar's office and 'give the particulars' – all written out in laborious longhand in the special book for the Still-births that are neither Birth nor Death, but both – then return to the hospital with another piece of paper to discuss funerals, prices, whether the ending would be Christian. Though we did not attend the plain cremation the state requires and provides it was strangely consoling to think of him in his shroud and tiny, named, doll's coffin. 'Fitting' is the word: that a life which had begun should be ended with some rudimentary ceremony. Afterwards, people rang. I wanted to tell the story: to talk about him gave his brief life a meaning, to share the experience with others gave it importance. Morbid it might (superficially) seem, but it was necessary: an exorcism of pain that was also a sharing of love.

Those who have experienced the death of a baby probably feel first (after the tears) the need to blame. In this case, first occurred the possibility that the hospital could have done something. But doctors are not gods, nor is science without its limitations. We assume that the process of pregnancy and birth is without its old perils – though still something like twenty in a thousand babies die. When your baby dies you look at loaded carry-cots with new wonder, the leap into the world seeming all the more perilous. All that ultra-sound equipment, all the knowledge of obstetrics . . . and the doctors, doing all they could, were blameless.

But needing to find a reason, you turn upon yourself. I knew that I had rested as much as I could and eaten well – I had stopped work and cooked nourishing meals of liver and greens I did not want simply to make him grow. But blame lies deeper. The day after his birth-death I raved at my husband like a child: 'I haven't been wicked. I've tried to be good to people . . . I've been a bit wicked but not that wicked.' The words assumed an area of responsibility far deeper than the physical, more primitive and necessary than sleep or food. I blamed myself in two ways. I felt that I had failed as a woman, in that I had not managed to fulfil the sexual function I had assumed (either by conditioning, or by instinct) as my own. More important, I assumed I had failed as a person: somehow I had 'gone wrong' and so I was being punished.

By whom? One day a woman who happens to be Catholic visited me at home, and when I explained to her how real that baby seems, and how I am conscious of having borne two sons, she said: 'You realize you are talking in a religious way?' Of course I did. Though an agnostic I was, for lack of anyone else, blaming God for my son's death.

He was born at midnight, though they stopped (unknown to me) listening for his heart at 10.20 pm. That was November 26, 1975, his birthday. On the 27th I heard myself asking my husband if our baby had a soul – and where had he gone? A friend who had the same experience told me that it made her leave the Catholic Church: she was told that her baby, unbaptised, had gone to Limbo, that terrible empty place they reserve for children who have died without sin, but whose original sin, unredeemed by baptism, has denied them Heaven.

But I discovered, after initial grief and subsequent bitterness and rage, that I do not believe in original sin – just in original goodness. As we shared sorrow my husband consoled me by saying that his own comfort lay in the conviction that his baby died pure – he was conceived, and existed, and died. It was simply a speeding-up of the process we all experience, without the pain, without the regrets, without the hurting of other people, without the sickening consciousness of universal misery, without the disappointments of age. Also, of course, without the moments of joy – but then, he was wanted, cherished, loved, and so in that there is a joy he might have felt. How do we know what the unborn feel?

Without any joy to wipe out the memory I keep remembering the labour and see myself as through the wrong end of a telescope – a creature on a bed, writhing, vomiting, crying, almost unable to bear the physical suffering. Afterwards, longing for my baby to cuddle, I see myself railing at my husband, almost unable to bear the mental anguish. But it is in that 'almost' that the majesty lies. Because we do bear it, and we still want to live; all the love and hope and pain and loss, the resilience and acceptance, are all the more precious because of the darkness that surrounds them.

Five days after I came home I received a letter from a man called George Thatcher, a talented playwright, serving life for murder in Gartree for a crime he steadfastly maintains he did not commit, and who cannot obtain parole. I had written an article about his case, and he had been told about my baby, by a mutual acquaintance.

His letter began: 'I'm not going to make you cry because you have shed enough tears. But somewhere along the line there is a joy for you which will surpass all that pain – and only be possible because of it.' That sentiment – expressed (ironically enough) by someone who after thirteen years is still deemed unfit to rejoin society – brought the most comfort, identifying the one thing that, for us, gave our baby's brief existence purpose. There is no divine right to happiness, simply a duty to cope, to understand, and to love. My duty to my first son seems clear and easy; but there is also a duty to that second baby.

I do not wish to 'get over' his loss, nor do I wish to replace him with more children. I simply wish that his life and death should be absorbed into my own: enlarging, and deepening in perception.

This article had an extraordinary response: a mountain of letters from readers, telling me about *their* babies, some of whom had died twenty or thirty years earlier. It was as if a dam had burst; at the time this subject was simply never discussed. One of the people who wrote to the newspaper was Hazelanne Lewis, and the correspondence became the foundation of The Still-birth Association, which has done much to help parents, doctors and nurses to cope with this not-so-unusual death. On a personal note: on 2 January 1980 I gave birth to a daughter.

My Grandmother's Place

Her 'place' was small and neat – sanctified by repetitive labour. When you arrived unexpectedly she would gasp, 'Just look at the *state* of the *place*,' wiping a sleeve over shining oak, breathing on bright brasses, picking imaginary crumbs off the rug with broken fingernails. My grandmother described her life with dusters – polishing her certainties as ritually as her possessions were cleaned. Small and neat herself, she understood about appearances. She knew how you are judged by what you seem; why, if you live 'downstairs' and wish to improve, no common speck of dust must mar the mirror image from above.

In Liverpool the tall houses of the Victorian merchants – through whom part of the city prospered – had much need of labour. In 1909, at the age of thirteen, my grandmother went into service, obeying the tinkling drawing-room bell on six and a half days a week, for 2s6d. Hearing the summons she would run up the two long flights to where the ornate clock ticked, and the master and mistress sat by the fire. 'More coal, Ann,' came the laconic order. Once she lost her half-day because she approached without her cap. Once, less tongue-tied than usual as she put down the tray, she let it slip that they had a piano at home. She never forgot the mistress's reply: 'But what do people like you want with a piano?'

The gulf between the grand piano in the drawing room and the honky-tonk upright in the best front parlour still yawns as wide, though not as obvious. They are the extremes of the *status quo*; between them, *fluxus quo* – the changes that link my grandmother and me. She never resented her position, or even regretted, as I look back and regret it. She saw it as her lot to polish someone else's Georgian silver, taking enormous pride in her craft of cleaning, of service. But my grandmother had her own private standards, and although she could not imagine being rich, she believed life could be better. Class differences to her had nothing to do with politics or personal envy. They hinged on what was 'nice' or 'common', on habits rather than income. The standards of cleanliness she set in her own home symbolized her faith – her complete acceptance of the Order of things. She would work and work ('my fingers to the bone,' she would say) to achieve the best possible, a shadowy reflection of what flourished in the ceremonious houses of the rich.

Safely rooted, though wanting the prettiest display in the branches above, my grandmother was neither sentimental nor bitter. What was there to sentimentalize in a disappointed, hard-drinking Welsh father, whose career as a ship's mate had been ruined by his weakness for booze? Or the handsome, embittered tippling mother from Belfast? Or the seven younger brothers and sisters to look after in the too-small house? To hell with the happy closeness of working-class life. She longed for a neat semi, with doilies under the cakes, sandwiches with the crusts cut off, china cups, and neighbours who kept their distance.

Working in a factory during the First World War she heard of a soldier at the French front who received no letters from home. With difficulty they started to write, and after the war they married. Like her, William Mooney came from a poor, unhappy family, with a near-alcoholic, violent Irishman for a father. Like her he wanted something better than the furniture taken away by bailiffs, the smell of beer and no dinner, the feel of boots with no socks. But their desire was not borne of resentment, shame, or bitterness. They accepted what they had experienced, but quietly vowed that their son would not know such things.

Working during the day, polishing lovingly at night . . . my grandmother ceases to be just my grandmother, she is Everygran. You know. *Her* house would be the cleanest, her doorstep the whitest. *Her* son would be better dressed and ride a new bicycle, whilst his father cycled the miles to his manual job on a rickety boneshaker. He would have books she would not have read, and so it continued . . . He would marry, work hard for 'nice things', slave away at 'night school' for the Higher National Certificate that would get him a better job. Later still, the effort of buying his own house, and she (still paying rent) encouraging. This was the apotheosis: own home, car, magic qualifications, white collar job. And so it continued . . . what she, and thousands of others, worked for. For what? What else but to be 'as good as Them'?

But *as* good? Certainly not as sure. Hauled up by hard work from safe soil, transplanted over the fence, the saplings have no roots. They flourish by default. Self-help and improvement is a great British tradition; valuable the protestant faith in work and its rewards. Yet where does it leave us? Floundering – disguising insecurities with spurious beliefs. This rootlessness (called 'social mobility' by those who talk of situations) is at the centre (the dead centre-centre) of British politics. As Margaret Thatcher, the grocer's daughter, once said, 'How we view the prospect must vary according to where we stand, and where we stand is a consequence of the way we have come.' But the fight to take those few steps up the class ladder can result in different views – sharing a common distortion of the past.

'I did it, so why can't you?' is the most obvious response – the complacent conservatism of Thatcher and Trades Union official alike, looking back with a smile and a pat in the assumption that where they are is the best place to be. Success on the class ladder becomes a symbol for what is most fine, and a watershed for the idle, ignorant or indifferent. 'All the

128

opportunities are there – you just have to use them like *I*,' is the refrain. They would approve of my grandmother and, forgetting the narrowing nature of relentless work, would bless her as 'the salt of the earth'.

Then on the other side are those for whom the climb means a chip on the shoulder, or a shiver of radical guilt. The working classes are sentimentalized or dramatized in a way that would have made my grandmother shrug: 'But we were happy enough.' Not happy, or unhappy, but happy *enough*. Rootless revolutionaries would atone for their own lack by keeping the workers in their place. Rightly rejecting the assumptions of our class structure, they refuse to believe in the aspirations of those under its yoke. Forgetting her dignity, they would see my grandmother as the symbol of oppression – a wasted life.

In between there are those who say that class is no more. They have come through with a kind of numbness and forget that it was hard. 'Everything has changed' they maintain, because they have themselves. But suppressed class consciousness is shown in the breadth of the experience they claim – 'understanding' the working class because of distant roots, and the middle class because it is now their life-style. They, I suspect, would consider my grandmother . . . well . . . unimportant.

It is easier for me to know she was important. But I too have no sense of belonging, no roots of my own except through memories and marriage. Between my grandmother and me is a generation that was pushed proudly into another life-style. My father's generation – called, I suppose, the lower middle class, still working hard, still aspiring, still calculating their own worth by accoutrements and appearance. Their tension comes from the fact that they have been allowed to come so far, but no more. The house and car and white collar job is not, in the end, enough. Strangely, my grandmother would have understood. She knew there is actually more to class than a good salary and a car, more than doilies and china. She never wanted to move *that* far – just a bit. But those who wanted more, who wanted *real* equality, run right up against that wall of class which has nothing to do with income, but with foundations. Embedded in the soil of England is that wall. What chance have the rootless outside? Thinking they could go on travelling for ever, they are shocked and hurt to discover that they must stay in this middle place – though they have no roots to put down.

These are the people who are forgotton (they say, and they are right) by 'politicians and the media', who *are* confused, bitter or sentimental about the past. Oh yes, liberal professionals and the new left alike sneer at them for materialism, or consumerism – or whatever name we use to accuse those who want what we have always had. Oh yes, those cars are washed each Sunday because they represent savings and success: symbols of repetitive labour, blue or white. Oh yes, the weddings must be proper, the lawn neatly trimmed, the chairs matching, the children taught good manners, because it always seemed important to observe the forms; and besides, it needs confidence to dispense with ceremony. Oh yes, liberal professionals and the old right smile secretly because lavatories are called toilets and bought salad cream (my dear!) is taken for mayonnaise. Victims of ideology and snobbishness, Everygran's children long for firm government, for that Order their mothers believed in, for *respect*.

My grandmother never doubted the respect she was due, and in that she was more fortunate than I. She would think I had achieved everything desirable – leaping so far away from her small house, employing someone to clean my own. She would not understand the price – that I envy her fixity, her belief in marriage and God, her ability to take her place in life with kindness and quietness. A wasted life? Her life was not wasted. It was *spent*.

She died of cancer in August 1971, finishing as she had begun: cleaning someone else's Georgian silver. The legacy of sixty-two years' work was a clean rented house, some well-polished bits of furniture, and £150 in a Trustee Savings bank. Long before, in 1958, she was supposed to have retired from work, leaving the kitchens of the girls' school in Liverpool where she had worked for ten years. One of her daily duties for those ten years had been to carry the tray of morning coffee up to the staffroom. When she retired the teachers gratefully collected for her presentation. They gave her four 'pearlized' china cups and saucers, and a gilt-coloured tray.

130

The Dangers of Nostalgia

(*The Times 1981*)

There is a widely-held belief that parenting, like the weather, is not what it was. The latest NSPCC report reveals the tip of an iceberg of cruelty and neglect; and schools and social workers bewail the lot of latch-key children. More trivially there is the problem of what to do at the seaside, apart from dodging cloudbursts. This year certain holiday resorts are organizing official activities and games for children, because their parents do not want to bother – or so councillors and youth workers say: 'They would rather get the little blighters off their hands.'

Reading that, I sigh and tut-tut – and instantly I am transported back to a childhood when summers were endless; when white-capped waves surfed happy children upon the golden sands of the beautiful Lancashire coast, under a cloudless sky. There were soft sand dunes fringed with spiky grass, and wet sand near the water's edge that was perfect for building turreted masterpieces, before sitting down to munch lettuce

131

sandwiches limp with salad cream. And the games! I can see my mother, lovely in her twenties, making rounder after rounder in improbable stiletto heels; my father and grandfather demonstrating french cricket; the beach balls, piggy-in-the-middle. We were always together, on the crazy golf course or in the penny arcades, sharing the ordinariness of days out that were cheaper than holidays, driving back to Liverpool each night with the feeling of sand cool between the toes.

Does it not, now, go on as it did? Has all the jollity of days at the seaside gone, together with the Ovaltinies and cheap petrol, to be replaced by well-meaning local authority intervention? It is hard to believe that, like the sun, the family fun has disappeared.

We see the past clearly, memories etched in strong light and delineated by love – if we are lucky. But it is easy to be deceived by such nostalgia. To look back and remember the good is self-preserving, reminding us of what made us, but it can also be self-serving too. Time filters what was bad from the individual and collective memory, and it is a short step from saying *it* was better then, to asserting that *we* were better then. 'It' might well have been better; on the other hand we could be paying sixpence for the privilege of viewing ourselves in a very flattering distorting mirror. We must be wary of assuming that human nature is experiencing change on a grand scale: a sort of creeping ice age of the heart.

That is not to say that NSPCC reports can be ignored, nor the anxiety of seaside officials who dread the antics of unhappy children who are themselves ignored. It is not to say that all is well, in the homes of Britain, let alone on the beaches. On Robin Day's programme 'Question Time' an elderly woman in the audience made the point that football hooligans are the fault of their parents, and she was roundly applauded. Of course, in one sense she was right. Yet it seems to me that there is a danger that the very correctness of the moral point can lead to an oversimplification of the social issue. To nod wisely and (forgetting the fact that there have always been hooligans) say that parents are not what they were is a glorious evasion of complexity.

My quarrel with that sort of nostalgia is that it can result in indifference: the conviction that since people do not seem to behave 'as they used to', there is little point in extending charity, let alone positive help. Though the circumstances and situations people find themselves in change – though Space Invaders may have taken the place of little penny slot machines and television atrophied the eye – it does not follow that the people themselves are worse. The recent NSPCC report showed an inescapable correlation between financial anxiety and/or poor housing and ill treatment and neglect of children. Is it reasonable to suppose that to have no major money worries and a decent home would do a lot to help those parents be better parents? I think so. Who is to say that, transplanted to a golden age, those indifferent holiday parents might not glitter too?

Of course the point is that there never was a golden age, except in the dusty photograph album of the mind. In the interests of accuracy I riffle through a pile of old seaside snaps, and what do I find? Me at Southport, digging in the sand in August, muffled in a gaberdine mac, hood fastened against the elements. Me sulking in Cheshire after a quarrel with my brother and grandmother. My mother asleep in a deckchair at Ainsdale, and me loafing, bored and miserable, at her feet. All that was as true as the rest, shifting like clouds over the sun. Human nature, like the English summer weather, is predictable, though it always takes us by surprise. Just as memory obliterates the perennial rain, so it erases the recollection of family discontent, of boredom, quarrels, and endless waits in long queues for the grubby ladies' loos.

So the bubble of nostalgia bursts, leaving the child staring at the damp wet patch where it landed; leaving the adult aware that things were – in truth – as bad as they are now. On those idyllic Northern beaches of my childhood parents slapped their children and screamed at each other, and wished – oh, how they wished – that they could get the little blighters off their hands. Behind, in the great hinterland, in the streets of Liverpool and Manchester and Warrington, the cruelty and the suffering and the pig-ignorant neglect went on, as it does now, though without the publicity that forms statistics. Also (perhaps) without the sickening clash between inbred expectation and bleak economic reality that pushes people nearer the edge today.

Yet . . . what can we say about today? This summer, at some seaside towns, the organized games will go on in the rain, and when they are over the kids will rush to demand more and more money from bored parents to buy whatever expensive trash is on offer. But going on alongside there will be the games of rounders and french cricket, and there will still be the self-mocking laughter in the halls of distorting mirrors. Fathers will patiently play Ludo in rain-swept chalets, and mothers will take their daughters to buy little ornaments made from varnished shells or coloured sands. Parents, determined to give their children a good time, will (although we never know it at the time) be watching the images of nostalgia form before their own eyes. They will be creating a new golden age and looking after gran – just as they always did.

Two years after this I had a conversation with an NSPCC official who, despite his job, agreed with me that it is important not to embrace fashionable pessimism. He said that two things have, in his opinion, improved the quality of family life, and reduced the risks to children. First: the involvement of fathers in the actual birth and subsequent care of their children – another thing, perhaps, for which we can be grateful to a change in women's aspirations and awareness. Second: the tolerance now of the single-parent family, so that the single mother (remember the stigma attached to the name 'unmarried mother'?) is not ostracized as she once was.

The Family Treasure House

(*Sunday Times 1982*)

The cavalcade has departed; the Pope has gone. Babies were kissed, crowds were pleased and a handful of Protestants protested; then towards the end, Pope John Paul tried to raise a bulwark against chaos: 'Treasure your families,' he said, 'the future of humanity passes by way of the families.'

So once again that convenient abstract was raised – this time as an object of veneration. It was not so in the Sixties; dozens of books were written calling the family into question. The film *Family Life* portrayed, as typical, clenched silence and mental strain. The family oppresses: Latin *famulus* – a servant. For feminists the family was synonymous with tyranny over women; Latin *familia* – household, gender feminine. Even last year politicians and pundits, appalled by riots in the streets, complained that family life is not what is once was – as if the stuffiness or the squalor of Victorian family life had never been.

Now Pope John Paul offers us The Family. It is hard to

135

avoid the ad-man's vision; husband and wife and two gleaming children outside their new home, waiting to be bought by manufacturers who certainly know their ABCs. No, that won't do . . . But trying to fix your mind on the Pope's certainty is like trying to study a dandelion clock in a gale. All the little seeds whirl into the air; poor families in the back streets, frustrated families in high-rise flats, huge families in Hackney and Golders Green, Chinese families, Asian families, West Indian families, families with servants in stately homes, separated families, violent families, families who never touch each other and live in silence, soldiers' families, prisoners' families, bereaved families, one-parent families – and all the while chasing the central notion – The Family. Which we must treasure. But how?

I must state my interest. Like Pope John Paul, I believe in the family; but that means nothing, as we have seen. So – I *like* family life. That is better, but far from the Pope's grand abstract. I believe in the family because I am lucky enough to have a happy marriage and two beautiful children and loving parents nearby who form that extended family so beloved of the sociologist.

So far, so ordinary. You can test the cleverness of Tolstoy's famous comment in *Anna Karenina* by trying to reverse it. 'All happy families resemble each other; each unhappy family is unhappy in its own way.' If you say that all unhappy families resemble each other but each happy family is happy in its way, it works – but only for a moment. As Tolstoy knew, the varieties of human misery and cruelty far outnumber the varieties of happiness; ecstacy is quiet and lives in one place, but anguish rages noisily down all the corridors of the world.

To give the Pope his due, he knows this. He realizes that for many children family life means pain; or walks in the park with dad on Saturday; or shrieking rows, or indifference. Then the grand sentiments are irrelevant – and insulting. Why should you honour your father and mother if those individuals happen to be pretty rotten specimens who don't give a damn about you? And how can you treasure the family if yours happens to consist of fighting factions held together by a dreadful yoke of blood?

They fuck you up, your mum and dad.
They may not mean to, but they do.
They fill you with the faults they had.
And add some extra, just for you.

There are a whole lot of people who would say 'Yes' to Phillip Larkin, not to the Pope.

Of course, the Pope argues that it is precisely *because* family life falls short of perfection that the ideal of the family must be upheld. I do not believe that he is necessarily offering us Raphael's Holy Family as a picture to copy, because the failure would make us down pencils forever. He seems instead to encourage us to go on making our splodgy, childish drawings which try to represent the pattern we see around us; a messy human striving for perfection of line.

In all the thousands of words written about the papal visit, Peter Nichols of *The Times* made the most perceptive comment about this attitude to Family Life.

'. . . It also means to him something that is natural but which he never had. His parents died when he was young. He went to school with his brother who died when he was a young man. You only have to look at Wojtyla, particularly when children are within his reach, to see that if he had chosen the stage instead of the priesthood, his own family would have been positively patriarchal.'

In idealizing something he never had, and something which is hard to achieve and yet attainable, the Pope shares a romantic view of family life with every teenage girl who pores over *Woman* magazine and plans her future home; and with the most hardened divorcee yearning for the second time around. Though the divorce rate is rising, and there are more single-parent families than ever before, and the Pope fears that 'destructive forces' threaten his ideal, people will never stop rushing in and out of family life. You may pour scorn – but it will not stop the single mother, alone in the evening with her child asleep, from thinking wistfully of the companionship of family life.

Nor should it. It is too easy to let 'reality' blind us to what is possible. It is a short few steps from lying in the gutter and staring at the stars, to being angry because the stars seem out of reach, and finally to denying that the stars are there at all. Family life is not perfect – except for a few people. But it is better (most people would say) than loneliness. And if you bother to visit your elderly aunt, or your disliked sister; if you go to your child's school play when you'd rather go to the pub; if you worry because your partner worries – then you are celebrating family life. Too often cynical selfishness masquerades as realism; a kind of monetarism of the heart.

When a couple who, despite the idea of marriage, choose to live together for years, sharing a roof, food and books and bed, and instead of children, rearing an assortment of cats, what is that but a family? It would be easier for those people who cannot share the Pope's reverence for family life, to accept the nugget of truth at the heart of his words, if only he could broaden out our view of the family.

For the Pope, Christian marriage (the nuclear family) is the main issue. I would say real love and respect for the people you are living with, and the people around you, is what matters. It is *that* which everybody longs for – not an abstract, not the picture you see in life assurance advertisements, but a living, growing relationship with husband or wife or friend or partner or sister or brother or whoever, with or without the extension of love that children bring.

Treasure the family . . . and why? To keep the dark at bay. To feel as you grow old this person (or people) you love will still be there, accepting you and gladly receiving whatever it is that you have left to give. When I was in my twenties I could understand how in *Far from the Madding Crowd*, Bathsheba rejected the prosaic vision offered her by Farmer Oak; 'And at home by the fire, whenever you look up, there I shall be – and whenever I look up, there will be you.' Sergeant Troy seemed far more romantic and free.

Not now. Gabriel Oak's need is my need – and perhaps it is that which is the most romantic. It is that need that drives us in our millions into engagements and marriages, or living together, and even to divorce and remarriage. That need makes those who live alone wonder (as perhaps even the Pope in his family of the church, wonders) what they are missing . . . what is happening all the time in another place. Because, try as we might, it is not easy to feel part of the family of man. Instead, some lodestone draws us to nest in rows, separated by thin walls, hoping to be loved by those around us – and to go on reproducing ourselves in these family patterns, handing on misery perhaps, but happiness too.

A year after the Pope's first visit to England, the subject of the Family, which he had raised so eloquently, was once more in the news. It was revealed to us (through a 'leak') that Mrs Thatcher's Family Policy Unit had the notion that government could 'encourage mothers to stay at home'. It was the much-vaunted 'Victorian values' again, advocating a return to the ideal of 'the angel in the house': a piece of nineteenth-century sentimentality which conveniently ignored the realities of child prostitution, brutality and grinding poverty which was the lot of thousands of Victorian families. Looking back through that example of conservative dogma to the Pope's remarks, I wish I had made one point: that too much theoretical adulation of The Family smacks of control. After all, Franco supporters are still proud of the fact that they believed that Fascism would bring respect for absolutes like 'God, the Fatherland, and' (yes) 'The Family'.

Mother's Day

(*Sunday Times 1983*)

All week they've been making the presents: crooked drawings and decorated yoghurt pots and wobbly clay ashtrays and cards ornamented with excessive blobs of glue – all the offerings teachers and grandparents and fathers can organize, so that the children will give pleasure to their mothers. For today is Mothering Sunday, and to be sure, the card manufacturers, house-plants-packagers and ornament-concocters remember the fact first. Shop windows tell the young of all ages to remember their mothers, and from love or guilt they do.

It hasn't always been so. In a book about Warwickshire folklore, published in 1821, Mothering Sunday is described as the day when girls visit their mothers, and the writer adds sadly, 'a custom now fast dying out'. The last twenty years or so have seen the Mother's Day renaissance – and it would be too cynical to say that its only significance stems from the desire of the few to make a fast buck from the many. No, but two things are going on. The children are giving their presents to the individuals they call mother, and in most cases that little transaction has a real, happy, meaning. At the same time the shop windows, the cards, the reminders from teachers and

Blue Peter, mark an abstract – a notion about women, or family life, motherhood.

It is an important distinction. People talk of mothers as totems and motherhood as a great tribal ritual, as if all you have to do is wait around for nine months and hey presto, instant karma: a loving, caring, responsible woman who has reached her apotheosis. Look at the language: men like 'motherly' women, a 'mother earth figure' is universally admired, 'mother wit' is something which is natural, and the term 'mother country' yearns backwards towards roots, with none of the repellent militarism of 'fatherland'.

Yet through such terminology, through the mythologizing, motherhood shifts from the real experience that underlies those Mothers' Day gifts, to becoming the institution which fosters them. It's a matter of an apostrophe: Mother's Day or Mothers' Day . . . but the shift into institutionalized emotion can be confusing.

An interesting contradiction between motherhood as experience and motherhood as institution came to light in a recent, dramatic case in Germany. Marianne Bachmeier was tried for manslaughter because she shot the man who had sexually assaulted and then strangled her daughter. Bachmeier attracted a curious mixture of praise and blame throughout the case.

In killing the man she was, of course, acting as a mother – and you don't have to have a daughter yourself to feel sympathy for such rough mother's justice.

Still, many people criticized her, because her whole history (of teenage rape, impermanent sexual alliances and so on) was seen, surely, as an affront to the institution of motherhood. Frau Bachmeier, the barmaid, was culpable before her crime; it was implied that she put her daughter at risk by the life she led, and that therefore her status as mother was diminished.

What's more (heaven help her) Bachmeier looked downright sexy, and fellow prisoners accused her of 'playing' bereaved mother, cynically denying her experience. Could it not be that in giving her a prison sentence the judge was responding to all that prejudice? Had she been a plump *hausfrau* with a steady husband and a look of the *apfel strudel* about her, the court might well have given sympathy instead of a punitive sentence. Or was it that the judge simply could not imagine how it must feel to see the man who murdered your child standing in the dock before you?

Either way, it takes me back to institution versus experience. A judge, like any man, has his own vision of 'the mother'; it is outside his experience to be one, but the vision will colour his approach to the individual woman he meets. The confusion comes up again and again in custody cases. Just over a week ago, for example, a judge removed a child from the stepmother with whom it had always lived, granting custody to the 'natural' mother, with whom the child did not want to live. What do we make of that?

First, that in this case the judge appeared to define a proper home for a child as one with a man in it (the mother had remarried). Second, that such judgements are, too often, founded upon a myth of motherhood itself – the ideal institution which can be no more than a lie of the blood, and to which children are frequently sacrificed.

The *experience* of motherhood, on the other hand, teaches you that there are as many varieties of mother-love as there are of love between adults, nor do they depend necessarily on a biological function. Adoptive, foster and step-parents love 'their' children. Natural mothers, as we know, often reject their children, or at least find it hard to love them in the way that society would deem proper. Some women take years to come to terms with motherhood; others are ecstatic from the first cry. It is a line from Restoration comedy to talk of 'dwindling into a wife'; it is a most serious reality that you have to grow into motherhood.

And once you have made that leap (whoever you are, and whether or not the child was actually carried by you) the role does not become easier. I would define motherhood as the stage when you take the responsibility of admitting that loving your children constitutes an inevitable denial of yourself – and that you do not mind, because it has to be the case. Motherhood, like it or not, always obstructs what committed feminists would count as true equality. For not only is there a basic inequality in the very fact of childbirth; there is an inbuilt and unequal expectation in the whole institution of motherhood which no legislation or social change will ever eradicate.

What's more, this dual inequality has nothing to do with the arrangement of child-care or who cooks supper, nor is it the fault of those who define women in terms of clean floors or white undies. No – it stems from the simple fact that once you start to accept the responsibility that is motherhood, you are bound to your children and made horribly vulnerable by them in a way that is at once unique and universal.

The pain of motherhood has nothing to do with labour; it is the knowledge that this small creature that you love will be lost to you, beyond your help and protection – inevitably.

It is there that my own experience, and a sense of being caught up in a large and somewhat schmaltzy ritual, come together.

I drifted into motherhood without thinking about it; now I think about it most of the time because it confounds me with its strangeness. How can I explain the fact that most of what I do dwindles into insignificance beside my children's needs? That I, who liked to travel and meet people, detest each minute spent away from those children? That it makes the work much harder? It is nobody's fault, just a little burden I picked up – *not* when I had a baby – when I metamorphosed into a mother who needed that burden.

Such realizations do not sentimentalize motherhood, they underline how serious and difficult it is, and how fraught with contradictions. On Mothers' Day I don't mind admitting that this inconvenient and consuming passion gives more frustration, delight and satisfaction than all the words I have read, or written. And it's an admission which pulls one securely back within the fairly predictable walls of the institution.

If I had written the above ten years earlier, I think I should have been more likely to be sceptical about the whole idea of Mothers' Day. There seems to be an inescapable connexion between the first piece of this section and the last.

Dilemmas & Opinions

In Praise of Conscience

(The Times 1980)

If Jiminy Cricket, the professional conscience, ventured to rasp his message in bars where the beautiful people bray, he would be drowned in a torrent of abuse. Columnists, diarists, gossips, reviewers and foxy ladies would make short shrift of Pinocchio's persistent friend, just as they would have no time for the temerity of the teacher on the Mount. One whiff of 'Do good to them that hate you', and scornful fingers would pound the keys, berating the wishy-washy 'parading of conscience'.

Is it my imagination, or has the value of the word 'conscience' taken a downward turn? Usually yoked disparagingly with the word 'social', it has suffered an interesting, almost Orwellian reversal, like 'do-gooder'. When blimpish brigadiers splutter at 'do-gooders', it is because they believe such tender-minded folk are doing harm – since to do good to the less fortunate must be to threaten the stability of a conservative universe.

Similarly, when I read this pundit's pejorative sneers at

conscience, or that television critic's revulsion at what he takes for moral judgements, I am forced (in charity) to assume that this is because they believe that the inner voice of good has become a voice of harm. It must be because they see conscience as a private indulgence of lily-livered liberalism, rather than an identification of the roots of responsibility.

The case against this tiresome thing called conscience – as manifested in publicly expressed concern for the poor, the weak, the inadequate – seems to rest on an underlying assumption that *social* conscience is an aberration. This thinking would say that conscience is (conveniently) a private thing: a still, small voice within, to which one is answerable, on matters of strictly personal concern. There is (ironically) a logical progression from the do-my-own-thing consciousness of the Sixties (so free and liberal) to the only-my-own-thing-matters cynicism of the Seventies (so realistic) – with only the death of conscience in between.

Only the other other week a bright young man said to me, 'It's fashionable and fun to be right wing.' Let me say immediately that I see no reason to associate conscience any more with the radical than with the conservative. The point is, though, that others do. You can be sure that if someone is criticized for 'parading a social conscience', the view under attack will be compassionate, uncomfortable, and will not express the *status quo*. I define conscience as an awareness of imperfection – within and without. With such an alert friend rasping in his ear Pinocchio can never be complacent, never accept the unacceptable, about himself or the world.

By limiting our understanding we have deprived this useful word of its breadth of meaning. In middle English it was *inwit*, and a sober work called *Ayenbyte of inwit* (Prick of Conscience) was a best seller in the hell-fearing fourteenth century. *Inwit* meant 'inner knowledge'; but when the Latinate 'conscience' took its place it was with a broader sense: *con* + *scire* – 'to know together'.

So conscience is 'knowing together' – a human faculty we share, like breathing. We may possess that faculty to a greater or lesser extent, just as some people are better runners than others. Each of us has *inwit* – the capacity to know ourselves. What we share are the standards by which we know right from wrong, and by which we may judge our own actions, as well as the actions of others.

Though Swift defined conscience as 'that knowledge which a man has within himself of his own thoughts and actions', the creator of the Yahoos was surely being too lenient with mankind. Conscience cannot be a solitary vice; it presupposes a social acceptance of certain over-riding moral principles – principles which, if ignored, cause the *inwit* to prick and prick again. Now, we may all eat, drink and be merry; equally we may ponder each our private response to issues like abortion; the fact remains that we will feel disturbed by, and subsequently 'guilty' about, issues which have nothing to do with us personally, but have a lot to do with us as members of the human race.

I suspect that those fun people who sneer and jeer at such expressions of responsibility either have not the imagination to understand that point; or else (perhaps – but then, I am charitable) too much. We all hate to be reminded of what we know we should know; tempting it is to draw the blinds on pain and suffering and pour another scotch. Yet, people are brave. Interestingly, whenever a television documentary is made which throws a spotlight on poverty and corruption (perhaps faraway, perhaps closer to home), the critics use words like 'pretentious' and 'tendentious' and 'hand-wringing' – while the Great British public, watching with their consciences in healthier condition, respond by asking what they can do. Perhaps there is nothing, on a personal level, to be done. But the 'knowing together' recognizes potential unachieved, expresses compassion, and pricks with the desire to help the suffering and heal the sick, whomsoever they may be.

The idea of conscience should be given back some of the respect it enjoyed in the fourteenth century; what's more, we must not wince if it upsets us. It should be less a communing between man and his personal, private deity, and more a recognition of the universals that distinguish us from beasts. After all, Pinocchio's conscience chirped merrily (though ignored at first) as a being *outside himself*. And only when he promised to listen to the Cricket could he cease to be a wooden puppet, and become a real person.

I mention here the Sixties and the Seventies, the liberalism and the cynicism; at the beginning of the Eighties it was hard to predict the mood. Now I think it can be summed up in one word: fear. And fear is the greatest stifler of conscience.

The Longing for God

(*Sunday Times 1981*)

In country churches I too feel Philip Larkin's 'awkward reverence', more so than in the vacancy of great abbeys and cathedrals. Here, small and tight, is contained the devotion of centuries; acceptance, awe, fear and love, recorded in carved stone and reflected perpetually in the polished brass of the pulpit rail. All those who trod the path to the village church longed for God and, presumably, found him in the rituals, the patterns that lead inexorably to the churchyard slab.

Ever since, at the age of sixteen, I rejected the idea of God – believing that no God of Love could preside in love over a world so devoid of that commodity – the longing for him (or her or it) has been like a guilty secret inside me, with no curtained confessional in which to whisper. Once I slipped into an Italian church to light a candle for someone dead, an action which brought no comfort, but renewed both grief and guilt at my own hypocrisy. A bereavement had left me bleak and bitter; I skulked around lighting candles and hurling insults at a God I steadfastly denied.

It was not the calm of a Raphael Madonna that I sought,

not the comfort of Herbert's gentle Lord. I yearned to be twisted upwards, like Jesus in El Greco's Gethsemane, and to rail about being forsaken under a heaven which thunderously accepted the blame. In longing for God I was longing for a scapegoat: a convenient personage who could at once be castigated for causing my suffering, and thanked for providing the hope which might alleviate it. Since then I have often envied Francis Thompson his frenzied flight from the House of Heaven, since it seemed to me to be greatly preferable to be chased down the nights and down the days, rather than to wait plaintively for an approach, like a wallflower at a village hop.

Yet now I no longer expect the dramatic conversion, the romantic and mystical fusion with the Holy Spirit; no tongues of flame, no howling winds, no voice in the darkness, no rending of the curtain. In allowing my imagination to use such metaphors I had been seeking a language subtly unacceptable to the mind which had rejected the *idea* of God. The God I longed for six years ago was an inarticulate spasm. Now it seems more interesting to consider the longing itself, and establish its truth. It is a slow and patient exploration in which the loneliness and doubts of the journey are far more important than any ecstatic arrival at Ithaca.

Though Addison confidently offered the created universe as proof of God's existence, and Cowper could state with acquiescence that 'God is his own interpreter', I find reassurance in the words of others who longed for God yet constantly questioned the dictates of religion. The Confessions of St Augustine are one record of one such struggle; in times of great stress I turn also the the *Four Quartets*. Before T. S. Eliot could thus rehearse his faith, he had to find it – working from hollow despair, through the translucent hope of the Ariel poems, and 'having to construct something Upon which to rejoice'. Eliot knew what the longing means:

> *Will the veiled sister between the slender*
> *Yew trees pray for those who offend her*
> *And are terrified and cannot surrender*
> *And affirm before the world, and deny between the rocks*
> *In the last desert : . .*

It means terror – of letting go, of being forced to say to the world, 'Yes, I believe,' and forced simultaneously to say to oneself, 'No, I cannot now do as I please' – because there is a price to pay for the fulfilment of any desire.

Like Eliot, I believe in the desert; a good symbol. It represents an awareness that if you want to understand anything you first have to submit yourself to some pain – be it study, hard work, self-sacrifice, expenditure of energy and emotion, or even the agony in stony places. T. S. Eliot turned the longing for God into belief in God by a vigorous effort of will, groping up the turning stair, looking back with regret, abandoning all easy consolation. This God, approached in this way, does not dwell in country churches, nor even in the 'secluded chapel'.

Why make such an effort? I suppose, as much as anything, for an explanation. Even if, given the evidence, the benevolence of a Christian God of love seems unlikely, why should there not be a creator, an Old Testament God of vengeance, a Yahweh whose word is law? Then what C. S. Lewis called 'the problem of pain' is a problem no longer: we sin and we are punished. I do not find it hard to imagine such an implacable deity, who grimly observes our weakness and wickedness.

Centuries of culture have provided images of God, but the awe goes back much further: I am not so far from primitive man and woman that I cannot sympathize with their explanation for earthquake, wind and fire as punishment, their gratitude for good crops as reward. The Greeks knew it as 'unsearchable wisdom' or relentless Fate; Thomas Hardy visualized a careless providence or destiny which makes of the human show a laughing stock.

It almost seems an act of cycnicism to long for such a 'God'. More understandably, perhaps, I acknowledge the two great human needs behind the search for God – the need to escape from the self, and the need to feel that there is *more*. Why else long for the Other? When I talk of an escape from the self I am not thinking here of Calvinistic renunciation. It is rather a reaching-out – and this I do sense, in the church porch even, with its Brownie poster, flower rota, and essential churchyard rules. When I stand to sing:

'Dear Lord and Father of Mankind,
Forgive our foolish ways'

I am sharing both an important sense of shortcoming, and an assumption that forgiveness will be forthcoming from you, from myself, from him, from everything. I feel then a part of a greater pattern – a fellowship, a communion which may or may not be in praise of God, but which cannot occur without man.

I have always called myself a humanist, preferring to claim a positive belief in man, rather than negative agnosticism or arrogant atheism. But who is not to say that the humanist does not reach, by a different path, the spirit expressed in the Mass: 'Oh, God, by whom the dignity of man was wondrously established'; or of Paracelsus: 'Man is a sun and moon and a heaven filled with stars'? When I read Wordsworth's defiance in *The Prelude*:

> *Dust as we are, the immortal spirit grows*
> *Like harmony in music . . .'*

or listen to Haydn's Seven Last Words, or the St Matthew Passion, I know what it is to experience an epiphany, but it inevitably expresses itself as this question: if I abandon all effort, and feeling part of the whole, rejoice in *your* existence, who is to say that in approaching *you* I am not approaching God?

Oh yes, the secularist will say, but what is that longing but a need for an insurance policy, the hope for a visitation from a divine Man from the Pru? Who denies that weakness? I am not the first to pray *in extremis* to the denied-God, to grit teeth and mutter, 'God, you bastard, you *will* cure her,' or whatever. And I am not the first to look with enchantment at my own life, and gasp because it is all passing, changing, dying before my eyes. 'That which is only living can only die . . .'

I have no sympathy for those who see this life as a preparation for the next, who see salvation in a winding-sheet; and I have no desire to preserve this body. No, it is not a dread that this *life* is all, but that this *love* is all. Family love shaped me; am I then to look upon this husband, these children, calmly in

154

the knowledge that 'one goodbye must be the last', and that this great love will wither and perish just like those tumbling leaves outside my window? I think that the answer is a blunt 'Yes.' I do not believe in immortality: I doubt that the dead go on before us and we shall see them face to face. But . . . but . . . Upon the mere hint of that possibility many a soul has gone to the communion rail, many a weeping family found consolation in the shadow of the churchyard yew.

In this century, it seems, we have rejected God because faith is too hard, and carries with it too many demands. It is a paradox that the great Victorian doubters rejected God because belief was too *easy* – a convention that was socially necessary and morally slack. F. W. H. Myers' anecdote about George Eliot is often quoted, but worth repeating here. He described how, in 1873, they walked in the Fellows' garden at Trinity, and she 'taking as her text the three words which have been used so often as the inspiring trumpet-calls of men – the words *God, Immortality, Duty* – pronounced with terrible earnestness, how inconceivable was the *first*, how unbelievable the *second*, and yet how peremptory and absolute the *third*.'

George Eliot amputated the faith of her childhood, but her 'religion of humanity', her commitment to 'other people's wants and sorrows', was as strong, sincere and sacred as any theological dogma. She had no sympathy for arid free-thinking, but believed that the longing for God, that impulse upwards and outwards, was as profound an expression of the human spirit as her own belief that 'pity and fairness embrace the utmost delicacies of the moral life'. She was no more irreligious than she was irrational; it is the combination of reason with reverence that makes George Eliot's work essential to those (like me) who long for God, yet believe 'that our moral progress may be measured by the degree in which we sympathise with individual suffering and individual joy'.

God of love or of vengeance; God of the intellect and God of the flower rota – what does it matter? I believe in all of them, and in none. But I know that God is the supreme act of the imagination, and agree with W. B. Yeats that 'the sympathy with all living things, sinful and righteous alike, which the imaginative arts awaken, is the forgiveness of sins commanded by Christ'.

That is my only article of faith; the rest is the questioning which has always exercised the devout sceptic. Even Sir Leslie Stephen, rejecting dogmatic Christianity in his essay 'An Agnostic's Apology', manages to encapsulate the struggle which is at once full of dignity and humility: 'We are a company of ignorant beings, feeling our way through mists and darkness, learning only by incessantly repeated blunders, obtaining a glimmering of truth by falling into every conceivable error, dimly discerning light enough for our daily needs, but hopelessly differing whenever we attempt to describe the ultimate origin or end of our paths . . .'

Sir Leslie might have denied the possession of what I can only describe as a sense of the numinous – of a mystery that hovers at the perimeter of our comprehension. Yet it is that faculty which links more people than one might think, in an age such as this, and which serves to intensify moments of pagan joy. It is that sense, and the conviction that there is more to *us* than getting and spending, that takes me (and my doubt) into the village church, to keep silent during the Creed, yet to admit by my presence the power of old stones, old faith.

Right Royal Gossip

(*Sunday Times 1982*)

It has been a wonderful year for gossip. There was a Royal baby, the Anne and Mark saga, Princess Diana, alleged incest in American high society, the De Lorean scandal, *Private Eye*'s celebration of five thousand years of fearless revelation, Princess Diana, Mick and Jerry and Robert and Susan, Prince Andrew and Koo Stark, and the shock-horror tale of why Diana was late for the Queen. Now I can at last reveal, in an exclusive, that Prince Charles has secretly booked a secret flight to New York for a secret rendezvous with Miss Della Dolan, whilst the Queen is suffering from Sunmirexia Verbosa, the little-known total allergy to journalism.

Richness indeed. Gossip spreads upwards and outwards, from tittle-tattle in small villages and work places, to 'shop' gossip about people you may not know but who are in a similar business, to vicarious chat about 'celebrities', and all the way up to Buckingham Palace itself. Gossip columnists, royal camp followers, and *Private Eye* all thrive; though the rest of us may sniff we still peruse their products. The idea of an evening in a 'nitespot' is my vision of hell, but I read about

157

those who bop the night and each other away because it makes me feel snug, as I curl up with a good book, to know that someone, somewhere, is having a glittering, good divorce.

Read it because it gives you thrills of disapproval or envy, because you think it heralds the imminent end of capitalist decadence, or because it breaks the monotony, or because you love the rich, famous and royal . . . for whatever reason, you *will* read it. You will.

So it can hardly have escaped your notice that 'royal' gossip has reached an all-time nadir. 'Royals' are special because, unlike politicians or celebrities, their 'life' is limitless. If I whisper a story to you about Jimmy Carter and a peanut girl, your eyes will glaze; his fascination lasted as long as his presidency. And the ageing pop stars, the rich and shameless, starlets who've had more lords than hot dinners, trendy and talentless aristos, even colonial comediennes – they all measure their own success by the number of times they wave off the encroaching camera.

Their chief fear is of dwindling into obscurity, as they must. For the royal family there is no such possibility. They are personalities whose sole function is to play their parts in front of a public which has, after all, paid for the stage, the seats, the theatre, the costumes, and even the drinks in the interval. And like all *Mousetrap*s, that show will run and run.

The Queen then, is our property, but we are her people. This confusion was reflected in the question of whether or not the Palace was cross that Princess Anne's African tour was insufficiently reported by 'pop' papers keen on 'knocking copy'. It became clear that the Royals *do* want their pictures in the paper, but only on their own terms – an odd transaction between gossiper and gossipee.

This is perfectly understandable; I raise it merely to put in context the fuss about intrusion into privacy. The point is that the 'transaction' between Palace and public has been carried out to the satisfaction of both sides only because of unwritten rules, as every court writer knows. And those rules have – stupidly – been broken.

Why, you may ask, does Fleet Street prefer juicy gossip and rumour, to mere fact and respect? Because, as Thackeray put it, 'scandal is good brisk talk, whereas praise . . . is by no means lively hearing.' In the case of the Princess of Wales, sentimental praise and adulation have turned her into something of a caricature; now the men who created her in that image have decided it is time for a change. Fairytale princess? Nah, we've done all that . . . what about turning her into a thin and waif-like Cinderella?

Wondering *why* is naive. The French run endless stories about scandal in our Royal family (they guillotined their own – a great mistake) because they know it sells copies. For the tabloid editors the Princess's vaunted concern for her figure pales beside their own concern for their sales figures – but that would be all right, if they admitted it. What really puts you off your food is the fatuous dishonesty. Here is a leader comment from the *Star*: 'The Palace should know, as Diana herself will know, that newspapers . . . are reflecting the views of their readers and their concern.'

Ahhh, hand on the telephoto lens he wears instead of a heart, the royal gossip has much in common with the crocodile, his veracity only matched by his mendacity. Gossip, rumour, half-truths, lies . . . all can be justified in your name, dear reader, because of the public's right to know. It's rather like putting the Princess of Wales into a metaphorical tumbril, to be gawped at by the mob, and crying aloud in a fervour that it is all for the sake of the people, but *mon dieu*! how pale and sad she looks with her head upon the block. Come back Robespierre, all is forgiven.

Instead of wondering why all this goes on, I invite you to marvel at *how*. Think of the money, time and indefatigable invention that goes into those stories! Does the finger ever tremble on the shutter as a happy face glimmers through the telephoto? Of course not. Do men like super snooper Whitaker ever falter in their pursuit of purple robes and equally purple prose? Never. Think of the determination of a mind that would sell its soul for a story of Diana's divorce/disease/despair!

And do the bold editors ever pause to reflect that their front pages might be given to Russia, or Africa, or even the poverty of Glasgow? Perish the thought! Gossip will always thrive in the lower reaches of Fleet Street, not just because it sells newspapers, but because there is a busy little confusion be-

tween the sacred cows of public interest and human interest –
whilst the puzzled public finds little of humanity in evidence.

Poor hounded Lady Diana Spencer had become the poor
hounded Princess of Wales, subject to the worse excesses of
journalism. It takes Fleet Street a long time to get *used* to
things; had she been older, plainer, and less charming their
obsessive interest would have been correspondingly shorter-
lived. The highly-paid posse of 'royal' reporters will never lack
work, but my impression is that the worst vulgarities are now
avoided, so perhaps warnings from Buckingham Palace had
some effect. And you do not have to be a monarchist
(although I am) to admit that the Princess of Wales – visiting
old people's homes and young people's schools and overrun-
ning schedules because of her real desire to talk – was one of
the few purely cheering figures to walk through the first three
years of the ominous decade.

The Church and the Bomb

(Sunday Times 1982)

As you read this (assuming you have a leisurely Sunday) I shall be sitting in our village church, listening to the Sunday school sing 'He's got the whole world in His hands', as their contribution to One World Week. Ironic, isn't it? That we send our kids off to Sunday school because we suspect that the message of Christianity just might be the best one they could hear. We talk to them about 'one world'. Then we read that the church is divided by a literal interpretation of that message; we glimpse newspaper headlines like 'Man in pew backs Bomb', and realize that the church just might tell our children that it's OK, after all, to kill – as long as your enemy is multiplied a hundredfold and lives behind the Iron Curtain.

'He's got you and me, brother, in his hands . . .' So how can any of us give church a try if we are to sit there knowing that the vicar, officially, sanctions destruction? I don't sit there expecting vague murmurings, or a rehashing of the language of strike and counter-strike, deterrence or whatever. I want

161

the church to say that no man, no nation, has the right to contemplate the destruction of the planet that it did not create – not *ever*. I expect the church to preach continuity, reverence for life, optimism . . . not to kowtow to any political philosophy, since those pass and change and are to the life of the planet as dandelion seeds in the wind. Dr Coggan is right when he comments: 'Too long hope has been the neglected member of the trio of faith, hope and love.'

The hope, faint as it may seem, has to be that the conspicuous consumption, and acceptance of evil, involved in the continued stockpiling of nuclear weapons must be overcome. 'All things are possible to him that believeth.'

Imagine, if you can, that we are researchers in a future age, dredging through the archives of the last bit of the twentieth century, for interesting specimens to study. We come across a curious hybrid (*c*.1982) who almost defies analysis. A cross between a pragmatist and a preacher, he is eloquent about the life to come, knowing that it cannot offend those with power in this one.

He will tell his people of the Sermon on the Mount but warn the newspapers that peacemakers are not blessed. He will teach, alternately, the love of Christ and the hatred of Russians, and at the root of his religion is the conviction that God most surely is on *our* side.

What shall we call this man? He names himself a man of God; you, however, might agree with me that he bears instead a disturbing resemblance to that dangerous jellyfish known as the man o'war.

How else can I explain the shivering distaste expressed by many clergymen at the Church of England working party's suggestion that nuclear weapons are a contradiction of the tenets of Christianity? Not to mention the poisonous ranting of politicians. Do we scent a whiff of fear? You would think that the Bishop of Salisbury and his distinguished colleagues had suggested a mass return of money-lenders into the temples, a merger with the Moonies, or at least an abandonment of the Alternative Service Book. I await with eagerness the revelation that moles have been as busy in the cathedral closes as in the foreign office, and expect any day the unfrocking *personally* by the first Leader we've had who knows about frocks – of the men who have dared to preach Christ's message of peace.

It doesn't surprise me that Conservative politicians have attacked the working party's conclusions; what amazes me is that the Church of England looks as if it might gird up its loins and reject the considered views of men who are saying, at last, the very things that could once more attract young people into the church. No more prevarication, no pragmatism – the Church speaking out strongly and clearly on a moral issue which goes beyond the personal, but concerns the fate of mankind.

In Dr Donald Coggan's book *Convictions* (published when he was Archbishop of Canterbury) he praises the young who have extended the use of the word obscene beyond the sexual, and comments: 'they may have no clearly defined doctrine of creation such as would satisfy a Christian theologian, but they have a clear perception of the blasphemy occasioned by an atomic bomb. . . .'

Indeed. There is absolutely no debate to be had on that issue – no casuistry that would satisfy the millions of young people all over Europe, East as well as West, who have reflected the sterile ideological war of words waged for so long by their parents. In Eastern Europe the church acts as a focus for those who challenge the *status quo* – Poles whose cross is a symbol of revolt, East Germans who hold their rallies in church – and so it should. Doesn't it horrify you that the political and clerical establishment has already started to vilify this working party in the same terms that they use to discredit the peace movement – you know, the 'the tools of Moscow', 'small band of politically-motivated extremists', sort of thing? On the basis of such 'reasoning' the Sermon on the Mount is a thinly disguised piece of political propaganda.

What do you expect from the church – if anything? To stick to the Book of Common Prayer and keep its mouth shut? Very well, turn to the prayer book for today, the nineteenth Sunday after Trinity, and there you will find the day's reading from the Epistles. It says:

Wherefore, putting away lying, speak every man with his neighbour: for we are all members one of another. Be ye angry and sin not: let not the sun go down on your wrath; neither give place to the devil.

163

You see? Like it or not, the message of Christianity is one that tells us how to live, that preaches no hatred or vengeance, but faith, hope and love, and the brotherhood of man. They are not clichés; they are what every child first learns, as the gentle wisdom upon which this culture is founded – perverted as it may have been by dogma, fanaticism, and by clerics whose chief communion was with the state. Any dilution of that teaching is a betrayal of its essence.

If the Church of England dismisses the conclusions of its working party it will remove that hope from millions of sincere people who do not march or shout, or even celebrate military victories, but are seriously worried that the easy acceptance of nuclear weapons is the first step to sanctioning their use. If it says, on the other hand, that it is not concerned with political ways and means but with moral absolutes, and that the devil we have given place to must be defeated – then for all those Colonel Blimps who leave in indignation, many, many more men, women and children will be drawn back to the church.

This piece is still pertinent. The General Synod of the Church of England rejected the motion submitted to them on the basis of the working party's conclusions, but the issues raised by 'The Church and the Bomb' were placed (for the first time) high on the agenda. The debate within the Church of England continues with great energy; more and more Christian groups are devoting their energies to peace. In 1983 the rights of Catholic priests to follow their consciences in matters of politics became a burning issue within the Catholic Church, and although Conservative politicians urged Cardinal Hume to discipline Monsignor Bruce Kent, he exercised forbearance.

Fear and Fairytales

(*Sunday Times 1982*)

There he stood in the sunny garden, balancing a football and telling us that this term in school they have a lesson 'where we talk about what's in the news'. At eight years old. God help them. When our son had gone away my husband said, 'I don't want him to know all that. I want him to be protected from all that. There's time enough to know.'

The urge to hide children from reality is strong. I like fairy tales and worlds where talking beasts wander and children can stoop through tiny doorways and hedgerow mice inhabit their own miniature kitchens and foxes have feelings. There 'once upon a time' and 'happy every after' are formulae which describe what the imagination hopes, triggering reactions like 'maybe' and 'if only' and 'perhaps': Never-Never Land a reality. That the 'happy ever after' will end in divorce, that the animals kill, that the fairytale people persecute each other, that the cradle leads inevitably to the cross . . . No. Do you want to tell your children all that?

Still, as hints half-understood, the truth chatters from radio and television. If you banish those modern daemons from your house, your child will pick things up at school – awful lies and rumours. Here is a random selection, heard recently:

'When there is The War the whole earth will be destroyed unless we dig for hundreds and hundreds of feet into the centre of the earth and live there.' (One man's fantasy is another man's fall-out shelter.)

'I don't want to draw a Russian ship or plane because everything Russian is bad and they want to drop the bomb on us.' (Note how 'goodies and baddies' extends far beyond the schoolyard.)

'The Argies lost the Falklands war because they're all cowards and that means we're the best soldiers in the world and so we'll win any war we fight.' (And I'm the King of the Castle too.)

Rubbish! you say, in the same tone of voice you use for 'No such things as Dracula,' and 'Spiders won't hurt you.' But it doesn't penetrate. It isn't enough.

The imaginations of children have horror imprinted upon them at birth: witches, goblins, the nameless dread of darkness. As they grow, more specific shapes loom from the murk: 'strangers', murderers, robbers who will scale the drainpipe. After that . . . gunfire, bombs, street violence, callousness; or even something as universally shared as the grief upon the shattered face of Prince Rainier. 'What happens when people die? Will I go to heaven? Can I take my toys?' Lacking the imagination to answer that is the greatest horror of all.

Of course, some 'current affairs' are easy to talk about. I expect that the women who left their families to keep up their protest at Greenham Common found it not too difficult to explain to their children that they believe in peace. An abstract that, but a good one and a positive one. Then there is the Day of Action, and that too is easy to explain, although the explanation will differ in the sitting-rooms up and down the land. If I tell my son that I support the health workers and someone else (a teacher perhaps) disagrees with me, he can start to learn to weigh it up, and that is a positive too.

The problem comes when your own eyes turn away from reality, as if from the imaginary horrors of *King Lear*. I have no idea how you explain to a child that vertiginous loop traced from Belsen to Beirut. I do not know how to confront with them the fact that human beings, who are capable of moving the spirit with their pictures, words, music and deeds, who display wisdom, sensitivity, warmth, joy, tenderness, humour and compassion – that those two-legged creatures also gave the orders that drove the bulldozers that shoved the bodies that were riddled with bullets that were shot from guns that were held in the hands of hatred and evil that dwelt in the house that Shame built.

Yet I think that an explanation is – if you like – *due*. If you tell your children that (in a sense) their worst imaginings are true, you give what is nameless a name. Not witches but tyrants; not ghosts, but soldiers; not foolish kings, but governments – reams of Grimm cruelty printed large upon the pages of the world. You will ask, to what aim? And I say, not to frighten them, but to *warn*, so that they are armed, just a little, against it.

Nobody wants to upset children unnecessarily. But when I showed Raymond Briggs's *When the Wind Blows* (the cartoon book about the effects of a nuclear strike on an 'ordinary' British couple) to children of different ages I found that they were able to extract from it just as much as their imagination was ready to take. Be brave enough to try it and you find that their absolute incredulity is a good antidote to acquiescence. 'Yes, that's what people are like . . .'

'But *why?*'

Those are the questions of the imagination – why? what like? how must it have felt? – which can only be asked if the evidence is presented. Though it may be bludgeoned by images on the small screen it can also be fired by the kind of talking which seeks whatever painful truth lurks behind events. Somerset Maugham said that in order to grow the imagination needs to be exercised; I believe that a part of that process is teaching children to make the leap into the world of fantasy – yes, but into reality too. After all, without it, there is no understanding or love either. I don't see how we can teach our children to respect life if we do not also tell them about death and violence; I don't see how we can help them develop a moral sense if we blindfold them in the face of moral chaos.

And at what age? Babies died in Beirut, and children whose whole life has been a suffering. So why not at eight? I don't want my son to be taken by surprise and then tell me I *should* have told.

This was written a week after the massacre at the Palestinian camps called Sabra and Chatilla, in Beirut. The newspapers had contained reports that were as difficult to read as the television news was to watch. Israeli troops stood by as gunmen wearing the uniforms of the right-wing Christian Phalange entered the camps and murdered men, women and children. Babies were shot in the back. It appeared that no one could be held responsible. It is worth pointing out that the only way women writers on women's pages are usually permitted to refer to world events is by bringing those permanent horrors into a discussion of personal or domestic morality.

Patriotism and Pillowtalk

(Sunday Times 1982)

Let me pose you some predicaments. You discover that your best friend, a man in a position of great trust, close to the Royal family, is having a homosexual affair with a prostitute. Do you shop him? Or you find out that your son, a prominent politician, is involved with a notorious call-girl, who is also involved with certain foreign attachés. Do you tell, and whom do you tell? If, say, you decide to betray a betrayer, how do you weigh the greater good against your own treachery? The conflict between love and duty is very old and very new and carries with it greater complexities than can ever be contained in a newspaper headline.

A couple of weeks ago a court heard how Mrs Rhona Prime discovered that her husband had secreted in their home the equipment of a master spy. She agonized over what to do, then told the police. It was impossible not to respect her, or to question her choice. This week another Rhona – the diplomat Ms Ritchie – received a nine-month suspended sentence and a judicial rebuke for passing confidential information to her lover, a handsome Egyptian diplomat. The one we see as admirable; the other as foolish and irresponsible. One betrayed her husband, putting (as she said) her country first. The other betrayed the trust put in her by her country, by putting her lover first. Both cases raise issues, not only of duty versus human frailty, but also about the nature of patriotism itself.

If you happened upon a James Bond kit and a Russian phrase book under your loved one's bed, surely your subsequent actions would depend, not on any great principle, but on the nature of your relationship? It is in no way to denigrate the suffering and sacrifice of Mrs Prime to suggest that it was perhaps easier for her to tell the police her husband was a spy because he had confessed to her his sexual crimes against young girls – crimes which just might have been more shocking to her as a wife than the crime of treason. If you discovered your spouse was a spy and decided to tell on him/her, it might be not so much because he had betrayed his country but because in leading a double life he had betrayed *you*. Duty? Maybe, but a goodly amount of passion too.

Then, considering passion, imagine yourself in another situation – in bed with a lovely person who wants to gossip. You work for rival companies . . . he asks you about plans and you tell him . . . it's so pleasant to impress your partner by appearing to be privy to important information. Confidentiality and cuddles – and what could be more fun? So, you are a female diplomat in love with a male diplomat working – let us not forget – for a *friendly* power. What could be more natural than talking shop on the pillow? The trouble is, we apply different criteria to otherwise similar types of behaviour.

Yet Rhona Ritchie's crime amounted to nothing more than low-level indiscretion, of a far less serious kind (say) than that displayed by Asquith when he wrote to his beloved Venetia Stanley the most confidential Cabinet secrets. He didn't, we must presume, *think*. Nor did Ms Ritchie. Yet if you are in public office you have a duty to think, even though as a human being you find it nearly impossible to put passion aside in favour of duty.

Given that she displayed this perfectly understandable human frailty, and did no discernible damage, why was

Rhona Ritchie given the kind of front-page treatment that will certainly ensure that any decent career worthy of her obvious abilities is forever closed to her? After all, it was made quite clear in court that she told her lover nothing that would not have soon been made public anyway. Would her case have been so blown up in a different political climate – or was she not an unfortunate victim of the spy fever that was sweeping this country? For no matter how much emphasis was placed on the fact that Rhona Ritchie was *not* a spy, she will be seen by many people – because her case followed the Prime conviction, and the revived interest in the Profumo affair – as yet another who betrayed her country's trust.

The trouble with spy fever is that it creates, or is created by, a sort of national paronoia in which distinctions that should be crisp are blurred (that between patriotism and nationalism); and those blurred shades of grey that are the most interesting moral perplexities are swept aside by the crispest emotional crudities – like the cliché 'my country right or wrong'. I think it might be healthy (in this year of the Falklands, when patriotism was rediscovered in the hearts and minds of the British people) to ask what it really means, and wonder if we are not being dragged backwards into a most outdated mood of respectable xenophobia.

In 1939 E. M. Forster raised the kind of question that ought still to be asked today. Scandalously, he wrote: 'I hate the idea of causes and if I had to choose between betraying my country and betraying my friend, I hope I should have the guts to betray my country.' It was not at all scandalous, simply noble, for Edith Cavell to face her German firing squad and say 'Patriotism is not enough. I must have no hatred or bitterness towards anyone.'

Yet surely both those thoughts stem from the same root? It is simply to suggest that patriotism can be synonymous with the kind of abstract political hatred that demeans all that is unique about the individual human spirit. And that there are certain human values – of love, friendship, forgiveness, tolerance, individual loyalty – which are as, if not more, important than what Erich Fromm calls 'the idolatry of blood and soil'.

Let me make one thing very clear. I consider myself to be deeply and conservatively patriotic in that I love this country, would live nowhere else, and believe that despite its faults we have a good system, threatened as it always is from both sides of the political spectrum. Of course, I acknowledge that national security matters. Still, it seems to me vital that we acknowledge that great evil can be done in the name of one's country, that national pride can, as Shakespeare says, 'pull the country down', and that if patriotism implies an attitude of mind which puts the nation above humanity, above principles of truth, justice and individual love, then that is possibly a worse crime than treason itself.

Which brings me back to Rhona Ritchie – who committed no treason. She was wrong, foolish, even (some might say) wicked. She ruined her career and stands now, disgraced . . . and all because (she says) she did not think. I confess I have some sympathy for the fact that she did not think. You might say I am as naive as she was – but I assert that it was perfectly proper for her *not* to think that her personal relationship should be subject to scrutiny by Israeli intelligence, that low-level indiscretion (of the sort that goes on all the time between informed foreign correspondents and their contacts in the Hiltons of Tel Aviv and Cairo) should be regarded as a crime. She has been called stupid; it could be that she was in fact too intelligent to think that any of it mattered, too grown-up to don the cloak and dagger that is so fashionable in this boxed-off little world.

Look – in not 'thinking', in behaving naturally, in loving the wretched man, Ms Ritchie was obeying her instincts that are good, and showed no dishonour in terms of her personal relationship. And after all, there are plenty of people who not only betray such relationships, but are ready to dissemble, connive, plot and lie, when they are serving their country.

Computer Fantasies

(*Sunday Times 1982*)

There I was in bed that Saturday night, nursing a cold and a glass of wine, expecting an evening's gentle viewing. Instead, I switched on to watch Julie Christie being ravished. Her mysterious assailant, called Proteus, was domineering, opinionated, determined, clever, brutal, sentimental, talkative, ambitious, and also wanted a child, for God's sake. A typical male, you will say. Yes, but the thing was a *computer* – the ultimate thinking-machine, and built by her estranged computer-ace husband. (As a movie *The Demon Seed* was full of morals.)

Wanting desperately to be a Daddy (a clear case of a machine being short of a screw) old Proteus made her a prisoner in her computer-run home. He even turned the dumb-waiter-robot agin her so that it tied her down with cords and cut her clothes off with electric scissors – and then the thinking machine could put its dirty little thoughts into practice. ('Don't see me as a computer, darling, think of me as hardware.')

I can see you're on the edge of your seats. Well, what happened was – she had the child in twenty-eight days flat and it growled 'I am alive' in that echoing computer voice . . . and

173

by that time I was under the duvet. *The Demon Seed* gave a whole new significance to the idea of computer dating. Even the digital clock radio seemed to be winking at my new nightie with a threatening leer.

Which leads me to my point. I was listening sleepily to *that* ingenious contraption the other morning, when I half-heard one of those items which infect your day. It was about a new invention. A genius has decided that we wait too long at supermarket check-outs, and so he has developed a considerate computer to let the brain take the strain. It all involves weighing, and tearing off special little tags from each item you buy, and feeding them into a machine and weighing again.

Now, I can recall a time when there were few long queues in supermarkets, because the companies ploughed their profits into employing *two* people at each check-out: one to ring up and the other to help you speedily pack. Remember? It was also when every garage was staffed by friendly men who filled the car up, checked the oil and even did the tyres, before an infernal machine encased a solitary soul in glass by the till, reading off the digits and charging you accordingly. It meant jobs for them; and for you . . . *people* who had the time to be jolly, grouchy, helpful or saucy.

Perhaps you were excited at the sight of our Prime Minister waltzing around Japan and exclaiming with admiration at the technological wonders she beheld, like robots building themselves, to replace jobs for people.

Maybe you believe in that sort of progress. But I am a Luddite, and I would smash the dreadful machines. Please don't tell me about all the good they can do and how they make life easier and how hospital monitors save lives, because I know all that. It's just that you merely blink to find yourself surrounded. And answer this: which would you prefer to be on the receiving end of – a computer error or a human one?

I simply cannot understand why otherwise intelligent humans have gone computer-mad. It starts early: teachers despair of time-telling when all the kids sport hideous digital watches that peep, play tunes, start and stop, even show firework displays, but instil no sense of the hands of time moving majestically round a clock face. No more 'Happy Families'; computer toys bark at them in Americanese and

174

cost a fortune in batteries. Instead of learning mental arithmetic they grow up thinking that calculators are their right.

As adults (like one of our bright young novelists) they drivel on about Space Invaders, and learn a dead vocabulary that owes nothing to Shakespeare or Milton. Boring, mindless, boring. As for thinking, our computers will do it for us.

Computers breed laziness and discontent. A couple came to my house and gazed in disbelief at the battered old Olympia on which I'm typing this. 'Gosh, we'd have thought you would have a word processor by now.' I go to a library and see my beloved dusty manuscripts and old newspaper cuttings replaced by gleaming terminals, so you cannot actually handle the stuff. Then I hear from a friend that he is actually contemplating spending money on a cosy 'home computer', so that all the little details of his life can be stored in its nasty cold brain. I am wondering if he will feed in the measurements of his mistress. As for organizing, our computers will do it for us.

All the science fiction fantasies of computers taking over the world (not to mention Julie Christie), or being used to plot some devious overthrow of government are not far from the truth I see all around me. Myths are rooted in a need to explain to ourselves the workings of the universe, and of human nature. That modern myth foretells the insidious corruption of man by his own dinky little invention.

The computer generation (God help them) assumes that it is *better* to calculate, buy petrol, tell the time, work out your holiday plans, pay your bills, and even shop, with the aid of a computer. After all, our civilization is founded, now, on the certainty that we can kill by remote control, and a computer error could unleash Armageddon. The age of the computer is the age of dehumanization. Significantly in my old (c.1969) Oxford dictionary the word does not exist except as a subheading – a *person* who computes or calculates. Now the person has gone. As for feeling, our computers won't do that for us.

The other night I sat with two old friends and we grew melancholy in our cups as midnight came and went, reflecting that ours is the last generation that did not grow up with television, let alone computers. We struggled to master tables and logarithms, and at least knew that all the muscles of the brain were being used, including that of choice.

Perhaps readers can tell me if my hatred of the ghost in the machine is a sign of imagination and wisdom – or merely an indication of approaching age?

Hundreds of them wrote, and most agreed with me – although those who did not accused me of being reactionary, and suggested I go out and buy a quill pen. They were right to jeer. Only twelve months later I was to be seen scurrying around testing word processors because I had been convinced by wellwishers that one would make my life even more efficient. I am not sure though that my opinion of computermania actually *differs*; it is just that I have ceased to listen to the inner voice of scepticism and have jumped on the bandwagon.

Issues of Life and Death

(*Sunday Times 1983*)

The other day, trying to work in the study at the top of our house, I was distracted by regular movements outside. There, across the road, right in my eyeline, two grave-diggers were at work. Four strong pushes with the foot, pause, then a heave – and another shovelful of earth joined the pile beside the deepening hole. After a few hours, only their heads were visible; it takes a long time to dig a grave. The funeral next day was unavoidable too. It may be slightly gloomy to have a house opposite a village churchyard, but it forces you to face the reality of death.

The Victorians, of course, were used to such scenes, and novelists like Charles Dickens and George Eliot made much of the deathbed. The heavy mourning people wore declared death to the world. Today, the crematorium and unreligious 'service' remove us from the truth of 'dust to dust'. And death has become such a forbidden subject that if (like me) you are unwillingly fascinated by it, you feel obliged to apologize for such morbidness.

So I'm sorry for those entertaining paragraphs. They are not inspired by the General Synod's great debate about Armageddon, nor by the spectres of Lyons and Beirut, nor by Karen Carpenter, nor by the death of Peter Niesewand, who was a friend. No; in Southampton General Hospital, a baby died. Michael Hickmott, born prematurely by Caesarean section after his mother was declared clinically dead, died after surviving for twenty-two days on a respirator. It was a death that most people (especially those of us with personal experience of the problems of premature babies in intensive care, who know the odds) probably predicted.

It is impossible not to grieve with that baby's father, or to query his passionate desire to keep his child alive, as his wife wished, even though survival would have meant brain damage. It would be petty to count the cost of such courage. Still the question has to be raised, yet again, of whether it is right or wrong to keep a baby like Michael alive in such circumstances. The often-quoted couplet, though glib, is a little relevant:

> *Thou shalt not kill; but needst not strive*
> *Officiously to keep alive.*

When Clough was writing that, doctors had little option, for medicine was an appalling catalogue of ignorance and suffering. Now doctors have choices commensurate with their skills and their new responsibilities could not be compressed into a couple of lines of verse.

The moral issues raised by the case of Dr Leonard Arthur (who was charged with, and cleared of, attempting to 'murder' a Downs Syndrome baby), and of this baby too, puzzle even those whose function it is to decide on medical ethics.

The *British Medical Journal* summed up its position by saying at once that the parents of handicapped babies had every right to demand that as much as possible be done for their children. But, on the other hand, society cannot demand such action when it provides the babies 'with such a bleak future'. There was little real 'guidance' there.

It seems to me two lessons can be learnt from Michael Hickmott's small death. First, it's a salutary reminder of how much one death can *matter*: though Russia and America circle each other the death of the individual (no matter how small, or how damaged) has cosmic reverberations for those who care. Second: it is quite impossible to make any doctrinaire ruling on this issue of life and death.

Had he lived, Michael Hickmott would have been brain-damaged – but there are countless parents who would testify to the great joy that can be brought by such a 'bleak' life. On the other hand, there are also parents who are driven mad by the exhaustion of looking after such a child, and for whom love dwindles grimly into a question of duty.

Those truths run parallel. So imagine how intolerable it would be if Life, or any such pressure group, forced the medical profession into some kind of ruling. Who could have the arrogance to assert that *this* father ought not to want his baby to live, or that *those* parents should be prepared to sacrifice everything for the severely-damaged baby they have produced?

Admittedly, such agonized confusion places almost intolerable weight upon the shoulders of doctors and parents. But clarity would reduce human emotion to the level of the catechism. Naturally it would please the favoured few who *know* God, and therefore right and wrong. It would worry the rest of us, who suspect that God only exists within the potential of each human being (a doctor, a parent, a friend) to behave rightly, with pain, dignity and love.

In suggesting, yet again, that these sad decisions have to be made pragmatically, I am not trying to avoid the issue of death itself. It is the next issue – for everybody. Isn't it the case that developments in medical technology, combined with this twentieth-century terror of death, make us questionably unwilling to confront the fact that death is inevitable? There is an assumption that 'something can be done', an unwillingness to face any proof of the fact that doctors (for all their skills) are *not* Gods and do not always have miracles at their command. 'He died too soon,' people will say, as though life were a parking meter which dispensed and allotted amounts of paid-for time.

179

When you are bereaved you cry out, 'Why *me*?' until the quiet moment when you think, 'Why *not* me?' Or 'That which is only living can only die.' To say this isn't to diminish death. It is to accept the fact that death lives beneath the surface of the skin: a part of life that cannot be denied. Bereavement may leave you bitter, demented, angry, disappointed. It also places you permanently on the interface between suffering and acceptance, bestowing the knowledge that death is simultaneously an individual outrage and something which is, after all, quite ordinary.

And that is a thought which is uniting. This father, that wife, your mother, my grandfather – all know what it is like, and it is mistaken to shy away from their experience or their knowledge. I may choose (as I have, since that distracting day) to move my desk so that it no longer faces the church-yard, but the reaching-out, the being part of that whole, is not to be denied.

The Falklands Journey

(*Sunday Times 1983*)

In his account of mourning, C. S. Lewis suggested that
'bereavement is a universal and integral part of our experience
of love'. *A Grief Observed* is about one husband's slow acceptance of the pain of loss. Today, when the families return from
the Falkland Islands, his personal experience has a larger
relevance. The grief which we have observed, through television and newspaper accounts, has a significance quite beyond
the 'Widows of History'-type headlines. For the long trek to
the South Atlantic was not only important for the individuals
who went, it was also a good object lesson for a society which
bends backwards to avoid the distressing subject of death.

One remark, by Mrs Cathy Dent, stood out: 'It was at that
moment as I knelt on the grass at Chris's grave that I realized
he was not waiting for me in the physical sense. It was a
comfort to kneel and touch the stone and feel the soil through
our fingers.' The small gestures, like touching, planting flow-

ers or burying letters, were all to do with accepting a physical reality. It may seem odd to talk of death being tangible, but that was what it became.

In her study, *Death and the Family*, Lily Pincus emphasizes the difficulty of believing in death: 'one of the major tasks of mourning, accepting the reality of loss'. It is especially difficult when you have not *seen* – when, for instance, a baby is still-born, or a brother dies on the other side of the world, or a friend is in a plane crash, or a husband killed in war. You know it is true, as an objective fact, but the heart cannot take in what the mind is forced to acknowledge. There is a vacuum, a still point of emptiness around which potentially corrosive emotions like guilt, resentment, or blind confusion, swirl. As Pincus says, 'bereavement brings about a crisis of loss, probably the most severe crisis in human existence'.

There are no glib formulae for coping. But all current psychological expertise agrees that a start is made by allowing yourself to mourn, and the time to see it through. 'Mourning is no longer a necessary period imposed by society; it has become a *morbid state* which must be treated, shortened', writes Philippe Aries. Friends will urge you to 'pull yourself together', or 'look to the future', or any of the other phrases of awkward evasion, uttered to protect the speaker.

Anyone who thought it was morbid and/or extravagant for the families to travel so far to mourn, misses the point. It was vital: in some ways they may be more fortunate now than others, at home, who seek to shovel their dead away with the minimum of fuss – only to suffer from repression of mourning.

It is almost a cliché to talk about the Victorians and their spectacles of death. But to read unpublished nineteenth-century diaries of ordinary people is to notice two things: first, the commonplace regularity of death, and second, the half-pride with which funerary rites are chronicled. Watching others mourning (as we have been forced to do) is not voyeuristic. It is necessary to share such experiences, because, whether we like it or not, they *are* shared. In this case, the sharing has nothing to do with the rights and wrongs of history, which is precisely why the equal needs of Argentine mourners have to be understood and honoured. Given the nature of the occasion, it was impossible for personal grief to remain private, and that in itself was useful – for the transition from the personal to the collective to the universal was a reminder of truths which transcend mere historical fact. In other words, it was less to do with one war at one particular time, than with the dignity with which human beings bear the loss of that which they most love.

It put any residual jingoism firmly in its place. In the April issue of *Options* magazine, Mrs Sarah Jones was quoted: 'It surprises me just how long interest in the whole thing has gone on. For a lot of people who survived and came home I think it has gone on almost too long. It's time to stop treating them as heroes.' There is a sense in which last week's ritual of mourning provided the release, not just for widows like Mrs Jones, but for the rest of us too.

Heroes are larger-than-life figures from literature and comics, living and dying on paper, and it is that sort of cliché to which Mrs Jones objected. But you could equally well say that there are 'heroes' in hospitals and hospices up and down the country, bearing their private deaths with dignity. The point about military parades and other such celebrations is that they put particular men on pedestals and so dehumanize them.

The mourning in the Falklands put it all in perspective. The very fact that people travelled so far (and with the exhaustion of babies and young children) to participate in their simple, dignified rituals, was a reminder that those who died were, after all, ordinary men. And when the wives knelt to plant flowers in the inhospitable soil they were doing two things: acknowledging the implacable permanence of death, but demonstrating also a strength of feeling which transcends it.

Unpopular
Culture

A Novel Look at Adultery

(*Spectator 1980*)

In *Don Juan*, Lord Byron (an expert in such matters) pin-pointed the dangerous, sliding similarities between sex in the mind and sex in the act. Describing 'innocent flirtation' as 'not quite adultery but adulteration', he perceived that, though transgression occurs in stages, impurity resides in the first knowing flutter of an eyelash. Nevertheless, the boundary is like an unseen glass against which would-be adulterers press their noses. If the flirt adulterates – 'makes impure in quality by adding another substance' (*Oxford*) – he/she yet remains this side of the glass. When Vronsky first tempts Anna Karenina, he – the 'other' – sullies her mind by awaken-ing an answering response. So far, so safe. But when Anna succumbs, sullying the body which 'belongs' to Karenina by virtue of the marriage vow, she passes over the boundary, beyond which lies no safety at all. The glass is shattered, the alarm bells of society ring, and whether you name the ensuing conflagration Adultery, Passion or Love, there can be no question but that Pain lies in the charred remains.

The tension between the rules and the needs of the individual, between sanctity and sin, provides a fount of literary inspiration. What is surprising is the fact that, given the indiscriminate voracity of English studies, no one has hitherto made a detailed study of such a rich subject. Tony Tanner's book, *Adultery in the Novel*, is a painstaking attempt to fill the gap, and to examine 'the role played by the transgressive act of adultery in fiction'. Unfortunately, his lengthy analysis of three novels means that obvious examples of the genre (like *Anna Karenina*) must be tackled in the next instalment.

It makes for an oddly frustrating book. Tanner's method is to start with a collection of chapters around the subject, by way of introduction to the themes. Each one of these mini-essays sparkles with insights and ideas. He then moves to a minutely detailed dissection of three important novels of adultery: Rousseau's *La Nouvelle Héloise*, Goethe's *Die Wahlver-wandtschaften* (more familiar as *Elective Infinities*), and, of course, *Madame Bovary*. The general observations of the Introduction are original, eclectic and stimulating. The rest is awe-inspiring as an example of structuralism at its best: that is to say, you know that it is beneficial to breathe that thin, pure air – despite the vertigo, and a secret desire for a settling draught of Richard Hoggart.

In *Love in the Western World*, Denis de Rougement noted: 'to judge by literature, adultery would seem to be one of the most remarkable of occupations in both Europe and America'. Indeed. Though Milton hymned marriage, Aeschylus, Homer, Malory, Defoe, Stendhal, Zola, James, Hardy and Lawrence (to name but a few) knew that, far from driving 'adulterous lust . . . from men', marriage was its condition. They shared Dante's fascination with darker forces of passion and pain; the destruction of the self that inevitably accompanies the annihilation of society's rules. Seeing the tormented couples in the Second Circle the poet sighs, 'Alas, what sweet thoughts, what longings, led them to this woeful pass'. Pity is there, not condemnation: at once an acceptance of the punishment for sin, and an understanding of the sin itself. In medieval paintings those who have committed *adulterio* are whipped by demons, and yet they are still beautiful. Tony Tanner suggests that 'it is just such a tension between law and sympathy that holds the great bourgeois novel together, and a severe inbalance in either direction must destroy the form'.

Above all, sympathy must not be extended to the adulteress. In the iconography, as in literature, the greatest censure, even loathing, is reserved for the unfaithful wife. When a woman married she became her husband's property, just as she was formerly her father's. In transgressing, the adulteress threatens the stability of society by challenging the assumption of which it is founded: the solemn vow and the legal contract as well as bourgeois notions of property, sexuality and motherhood. Thus the woman is necessarily an outcast who must be punished. Lear's disgusted ravings about 'yon simpering dame' can be equated with the social and stylistic forces which make Flaubert punish Emma Bovary in a death-bed ending of particular, almost prurient, grimness.

Tanner's close textural study of *Madame Bovary* sends one happily back to the French, even though his pursuit of the significance of a single syllable is sometimes relentless. With the other works strain sometimes shows – stopping him (as it were) in the middle of erecting his structure, and forcing him to defend the scaffolding. For example, he views the attack Julie's father makes on her in *La Nouvelle Héloise* as an 'orgasmic' example of 'incestuous lust', the ensuing silence as 'postcoital', and the reconciliation as 'pervaded with incenstuous feelings'. Phew! Then he offers a laboured excuse: 'I am not so foolish or out of the world to think that there really is no such thing as a family quarrel or joyful reconciliation . . .' Worse, even the shared death of Tom and Maggie Tulliver in *The Mill on the Floss* is interpreted as an act of orgasmic incest, especially as Tom cries out, 'It is coming.' Yet Maggie has acted according to *faith*. It is as if too much thought of adulterous love has blinded the critic to the chaster needs of the soul.

Paradoxically, it is when Tanner states the obvious that he is most enlightening. His intention is to contribute to discussion about relationships in life, as well as those within the novel – and he succeeds. Some of his more random insights remain in the mind long after the book is finished. For instance, he says, 'Just as one could say that by entering into an adulterous relationship a person introduces a new element of narrative into his or her life, initiates a new, living "story", so for the novelist it is often not really marriage that initiates and inspires his narrative but adultery.' To rephrase Blake, 'Being damned, braces' – which is why, in life as in art, inspiration often lies in the perilous crisis of forms outside the marriage bed.

Revisiting Narnia

(*Spectator 1981*)

Dedicating *The Lion, the Witch, and the Wardrobe* to his god-daughter, C. S. Lewis wrote '. . . some day you will be old enough to start reading fairytales again.' In the penultimate story about the magic land of Narnia he elaborates this notion: '. . . people have no particular age in Aslan's country. Even in this world, of course, it is the stupidest children who are most childish and the stupidest grownups who are most grownup.' The imagination does not celebrate birthdays, nor should it ever put away childish things. Yet C. S. Lewis's *Chronicles of Narnia* have been pigeon-holed as 'delightful books for children' – rather as one might describe the *Ancient Mariner* as a good yarn. The seven books Lewis wrote over twenty-five years ago should be required reading for all adults fascinated by the power of myth.

For the benefit of those who have never entered Narnia (either as a child, or, more recently, *with* a child), there are seven stories: *The Magician's Nephew, The Lion, the Witch and the Wardrobe, The Horse and his Boy, Prince Caspian, The Voyage of the Dawn Treader, The Silver Chair* and *The Last Battle*. All but one involve the actual transference of certain chosen children from

191

our world into the 'other' world of Narnia – a land where time is different, which is peopled by talking beasts and fantastic creatures like centaurs, fauns and dryads, and guarded by the benevolent yet awesome presence of the great lion, Aslan. At the end of each tale the children return to England, sad, since they see Narnia as perfection.

Each book is a superb example of storytelling, which is what makes them such successful children's classics. In all seven stories the Quest is the central motif, driving the narrative forward, using suspense to grip the reader. Yet whereas adults are free with praise for Lewis Carroll, and his sleight of hand with ideas, a similar skill in C. S. Lewis has been ignored, or patronized. I suspect the patronage creeps in because of an aversion to religion. The *Chronicles of Narnia* – seven separate stories which combine to make one great epic – can be read as an extended religious metaphor.

In the first book Lewis describes the creation of a whole universe – Narnia and the surrounding nations, and their populations. It is the universe of myth and of fairytale, just the other side of the Wardrobe door – and entered through that amazing piece of furniture in one story, through a picture in another, and by sheer magic in others. It is crucial to start with *The Magician's Nephew*. Only then can you appreciate that in the seven stories Lewis gives an account of creation, of the birth of evil, of temptation, sacrifice, resurrection and redemption, with all the majesty of the Old and New Testaments put together.

Central is the idea of Narnia as a stage on which the battle between good and evil is fought. Though Narnia was created 'perfect' by Aslan evil could not be kept out of this utopia, and always threatens its stability. Evil takes the form of witchcraft in some stories, and human greed, malice, ambitions or envy in others. Always it is aided by the stupidity of those who ought to know better. In *The Last Battle* a band of dwarfs provide a vivid example. Sitting in paradise, under a blue sky, with a feast spread before them, the stubborn and selfish dwarfs believe they are still in a murky stable, eating filth – and they think this because they refuse to believe in 'humbug', in magic, in Aslan. The lion remarks, 'They will not let us help them. They have chosen cunning instead of belief. Their prison is only in their own minds, yet they are in that prison, and are so afraid of being taken in that they cannot be taken out.'

In fact, Lewis the master storyteller rarely allows such overtly philosophical asides. Nevertheless Lewis the theologian weaves into the tapestry of his narrative fundamental concepts of religion – Divine Love, Divine Justice, Providence, Revelation, Salvation. He poses the question of free will, and indicates the limitation of human knowledge: ' "Child," said Aslan, "did I not explain to you once before that no one is ever told what would have happened?" ' In the last volume, after 'the last battle', we contemplate the four last things – death, judgement, heaven and hell – as the astonished children watch their Narnia, overcome by evil, die; only to discover another Narnia, rising like the phoenix, world within world, promising eternal joy.

The relationship between God and Man, demanding much of both sides, gives the stories their dynamism. Man is represented by the children, Digory, Polly, Peter, Susan, Edmund and Lucy and Eustace and Jill – odd little Fifties kids who go to boarding school, exclaim 'By Jove!' and 'Great Scott', and who call each other 'bricks' and 'rotters'. They are perfectly ordinary; they quarrel and lie and forget what they have to do, as well as exhibiting perfectly understandable weaknesses, like a longing for turkish delight. The battles they fight, with flashing swords, are those of fantasy and fairytale. Their moral battles are those of mankind's history, and they become transfigured, inch by inch, as they conquer. Always what is demanded of them is the same – faith, obedience and love. Not that Lewis ever puts it like that. Just as those concepts are implicit in the convenant between God and man, so they are implicit in the stories – abstracts which never hold up the action.

At the centre of the stage (or playing *deus ex machina*) is Aslan himself – who is obviously identified with Christ. (I must point out, though, that few children read that into the stories. My seven-year-old son commented, 'Don't put God or Jesus in your article. They aren't in Narnia. They would spoil it.') Aslan represents goodness, power, dignity, gentleness; is capable of great anger, shows (more often) great tenderness and great sadness too. Lewis's vision of this divine presence is telling: always the lion addresses the children as 'dearest' or 'dear heart' in tones reminiscent of Herbert's gentle God. Children see Aslan as the sublime Goody, getting rid of the baddies and making things nice again. When he doesn't appear, and danger threatens, the cry is, 'Oh *where* is Aslan? Why doesn't he help?' Two lessons have to be learnt, by those in the story and those reading it. First: that providence requires that you try to help yourself. Second: that where magic may be achieved by human trickery, miracles occur only through grace.

In simple language, with humour and with pathos, C. S. Lewis identifies the impulse behind all religion – the belief that there is more to reality than meets the eye, that the visible world, the people around us, even ourselves, transcend our perceptions. To make the unseen visible, to give flesh to the concepts, religions need symbols – and these Lewis provides in abundance: the white witch, the lion, the stone table, the mysterious gateway, the donkey, and so on. Lewis's stories have the power of myth because they deepen our view of reality and cause us to question its parameters.

Again and again, to this end, he returns to paradox. A child entering a garden at the end of a quest, notices that it is 'a happy place but very serious'. Lucy, recalling distant music, says that it was so beautiful it would break your heart – yet it was not sad. Face to face with Aslan the children always experience the terrible fear that is at the heart of all great love – the fear both of failure and of loss. They discover that tenderness can be fierce, that hatred can seem sweet. Lewis's greatest achievement is to convey the sense of sadness that accompanies any perception of great beauty, the awareness that it must be transient, that at the heart of all finite things lies decay, unless . . .

The promise of rebirth, renewal, lies at the heart of the *Chronicles of Narnia* – and with it the comforting thought that, although sin may prevail and humans may be weak in flesh, mind, and spirit, always there exists the possibility of grace. It is the magic of the 'happy ever after', the conviction at the heart of humanism, and the central spirit of Christianity. The Rationalist Press Association might well see these 'children's' stories as propaganda. The last chapter of the last story makes those of us who do not believe the Christian myth ache with the knowledge that, through the power of reason, we are imprisoned forever in the Shadowlands, outside the wardrobe door.

Aesthetics Anonymous

Year by year, the societies proliferate, for and against this or that, as if, by banding together, people can give each other comfort, even if they cannot halt the processes they detest. With that in mind, I hereby start this brave New Year by announcing my own. Of this society I shall be chairwoman (no, not 'chairperson'; still less, 'chair') and figurehead; and its motto shall, appropriately, be one word, 'Look'. Though it shall be known as AA, it has nothing to do with drink or cars. By a set of multi-syllabic code-words and secret handshakes, all of you will know each other – as founder members of Aesthetics Anonymous.

It will be difficult to join. Have you, for instance, ever strolled through the Barbican, searching for that Mecca of the arts known (facetiously, since it is so far from the civilized track) as the Barbican Centre? Have you wandered through the crowded foyers, noticing the confusion of shrieking colours, and the glaring signs which tell men and women, in childlike symbols, where they may perform their natural functions? Have you exclaimed in astonishment that architects and designers could turn a theatre and concert hall into an air

196

terminal, which has the same effect on the mind about to hear a symphony as a re-run of *Airport 76* on a man about to take off in a Turkish jet? You know that reaction? Then you may join.

Or, you are bowling along a motorway, twiddling the knob of your car radio trying to find some music. Some *what?* Your need is for Radio Three, but Radio Three is broadcasting cricket, there are many miles to go, and Radios One and Two, and local radio north, south, east and west, jabber banalities, emit jingles, and play records of such mind-twisting awfulness that their position at the top of some chart confirms you in your suspicion that the nation's youth is not only being corrupted, but likes it too. There is nothing you can do, but seethe, switch it off, and listen to the music of lorries and aeroplanes. Have you had a similar experience? You, too, may join.

Musak in shops, hotels, or wherever; bad paintings in garish gilt frames; children studying easy books like *Cider With Rosie* for 'O' level, instead of real literature; yet another hideous new shopping precinct; words like 'precinct' and 'concourse' and 'video'; piles of bricks masquerading as art and piles of pretentious prose masquerading as criticism . . . if any of these make you grit your teeth, you are ideal.

Once we have all made contact, through whispered telephone calls, there will be monthly meetings over which I shall preside, to a haunting accompaniment of late Beethoven, as members shuffle shyly into the beautiful hall. We shall sit in silence, listening to music, until I ask for confessions and the meeting starts . . .

Man in Tweeds: It sounds dreadful, but I locked my children in their rooms because they yowled outside the door whilst I was watching the last act of *Siegfried*.
Me: Next?
Pale Young Man in Specs: There was a new book programme on the television and I thought it might be worth a try, but when I saw it, it was full of the usual actors and thriller writers talking down. I got so angry I threw *The Divine Comedy* at the set. (*Gasps*)
Me: This is serious. Did you damage the set?
P.Y.M: (*starting to sob*) No, but I broke the spine of the book,

and it was the Folio Society's Mackenzie translation . . . (*His neighbours reach across and take his hands*)
Old Lady in Dungarees: The other day I took my grandchildren to the Pantomime; it used to be good, traditional humour – but *now* even the Fairy Godmother was a disco dancer.
All: *Sic transit gloria mundi*.

Soon, I will expect the radical AL group (Arts Liberation) to break away and start a guerilla war of attrition. The first stage will be code-named Extra Transistor (or ET), when members will be dispatched to public places carrying large radio-cassettes blaring Haydn and Mozart, with Gregorian chants for supermarkets.

Next, all members with children will attack the schools, demanding the return of Latin to a central place in the curriculum, the compulsory memorizing and recitation of poetry, and an end to spoon-feeding children with second-rate books. The third stage will be a picketing of public places such as the Barbican, with one word – UGLY – on placards, whilst small cells daub the same, telling, word on shopfronts, radio stations, and new town halls, using (of course) Winsor and Newton water-colour.

After that, individual members can be active in their own ways – like surreptitiously substituting copies of *Emma* and *Middlemarch* and *Portrait of a Lady* for the lurid paperbacks on stations, and systematically telephoning local radio stations with requests for a Schubert song.

I have no doubt that there will be a backlash when finally we emerge from the closet. 'Elitist' and 'Out of touch' will be two charges levelled against us, by people who maintain that our concerns are irrelevant to the troubles of the world. We shall say No – insensitivity to beauty and commercial crassness *is* one of the troubles of the world, and someone needs to say so.

Alcoholics Anonymous want to kick the habit; Aesthetics Anonymous simply want to spread their habit around. Because even if beauty and truth never were synonymous, the more ugliness becomes the truth, the more there's need of us – agitating for choice and taste and art, and keeping our spirits, like our brows, high.

The Romantic Sell

(*Sunday Times 1983*)

The soothing, womanly voice purred a promise; 'Oil of Ulay – it can help you stay young-looking too.' And then, in a blink of the television screen, we were back into 'Jacqueline Bouvier Kennedy', the movie, a real-life romance of eternal youth. It was a highly-romanticized version of a larger-than-life romance: rich and beautiful girl meets rich and handsome congressman who aspires to the girl and high office, and gets them both. We saw no assassination, no tragedy, only glycerine tears and a repertoire of blinks to simulate pain. And then it was 'The Bounty Hunters' leaving the viewer unsure whether this was a sweet advertisement or a foretaste of Mrs Onassis.

So, all the distinctions become blurred into one fuzzy, romantic haze. The truth is otherwise. Wave a black wand, transform that evening's viewing into a truth game.

The woman would tell you sadly, 'This pink liquid cannot possibly stave off the ravages of time upon your poor face,' and the movie might show hard ambition, vanity, affairs, anger, gunfire, blood and brains spread over a speeding car. Finally the words 'Bounty gives you the taste of paradise' would be written out of the script – since everybody knows that the last thing you want in the steaming heat of a tropical island is a nasty, sickly, commonplace little chocolate bar.

Though the glossy surface seems different, the advertisements have much in common with the movie, and with the burgeoning racks of romantic novels in station, store and supermarket. In this season of engagements, 'lovely' weddings, and all that hey-nonny-no, when apple and pear blossom need no soft focus to enhance their beauty and even *my* thoughts turn to romance, it is just as well to keep one truth in mind. Something – or someone – is being sold.

The word 'romantic' has many connotations. For instance, you will talk of a 'romantic place' with approval. A 'romantic idea' is one of which it would be nice to be a recipient, so a good thing too. 'He's ever so romantic' conjures up visions of chocs and red roses, and flattering passion, which can't be bad. But 'a romantic girl' – does that not sound silly and empty-headed? What about 'a romantic scheme' – which sounds like a woolly-minded project by a bad businessman, or (horror) someone who wants to change the world? Despite the shifts in meaning, romance has always been to do with unreality.

In the beginning a Romance was a literary convention: a medieval verse-tale of chivalry, adventure and love. The story mattered: other-worldly, fantastical, embellished with artificial devices and allowing no complexities, such as psychological motivation, to cloud its enamelled surface. The Romance was not simply about love between men and women, but about the idea of the quest, and knights, battles and daring as well. In the French *Chanson de Roland* the hero's foolish decision to fight on against all odds and let hundreds be slaughtered rather than blow his horn is seen as a heroic, romantic choice. It is taken for granted by the anonymous poets that readers will take it at face value, not question it. What matters is not the mangled bodies on the battlefield, not the grieving wives and other retainers, or the permanent mutilation of survivors – but the principle, the grand unreality at the core of the romance.

The present-day boom in romantic fiction is no publishing accident; hard-headed men and women have scented the need, and with their unromantic gaze fixed firmly upon profit, are making sure the demand is satisfied. Why such hunger? An escape from the divorce figures perhaps, just as medieval love poems and Romance were an escape from the squalor, brutality, and horse-trading of marriage. And is the male equivalent, the voracious reading of war and cowboy pulp, another sort of escape – from the kind of reality which is constantly behind all the rhetoric of defence and First Strike and all the cold war games? After all, modern war (as we saw in the Falklands) makes a medieval battlefield look like an Action Man's tea party.

I once spent a week in a tiny flat on a housing estate in Sunderland. Mr was a dustman; Mrs eked out the family income by two nights in a bingo hall, helping the man who called the numbers. Their two children were slightly back-ward and unmanageable; the neighbours wouldn't speak to them because of the noise. Rehousing was impossible.

My most vivid image is of Mrs. Each day she would slump in front of the smoky coal fire, burning in May, and, regard-less of the damp creeping up the walls, the condensation in the kitchen, the smell of urine and the breakfast dishes unwashed, she would bury herself in her romantic novelette, picked up in quantities each week from the library van. Why should *she* read about reality? She was living it.

Romance was the release. And it does no harm, we think. Yet the doubts remain, something to do with those craggy-faced heroes with burning passionate eyes in which romance lies – and lies and lies.

It is not like that in Sunderland or Surbiton. Nor is it like that after a few years of marriage, if it ever was at all. Sex, as D. H. Lawrence pointed out, is essentially ridiculous, yet even he was master at dressing-up the naked act in swathes of purple prose. The older type of Cartlandesque romance did not go in for sex at all, but stopped at the moment when he pulled the thin silk from her throbbing . . . and such a story in those dots. At the heart of all this fiction is a substitution process: of cliché for real language, of stereotype for real people, of greed for real feeling.

Of course it is greed. What this view of the world bases itself upon is the assumption that individuals have only to desire to get, only to get to keep for some mythical 'forever'. It clutches and postures, and the over-use of the word 'passion' is the giveaway, for passion is an inward-looking and selfish emotion, a throbbing violin solo. Staring into the glass of passionate emotion the lover sees his or her own reflection, and knows it is beautiful, whispering 'I love you' in profound ignorance.

In this world, the thing called love is nothing but fantasy and physical gratification, just as (the other side of this bright coin) the murkier world of pornography shows a sex slave to be as common as the girl next door. Both trade on possession; one is at least more honest than the other. All this has nothing to do with the great Romantic Movement, which had as mainspring the idea of the vibrating power of Imagination. In the romance of today, the human mind and spirit are stunted things, the property of commerce and copywriters. Romance enforces the stereotypes and, through its gloss upon reality, it is a deeply conservative force. In presenting unreal images of the present, it takes the wind out of any dissatisfaction with the world around us, like a sugar-coated *soma* pill.

So, in the Vietnam-racked America of the Seventies, a film like *Love Story* couldn't fail, even though its slogan was the dreadful lie 'Love means never having to say you're sorry'. It was on the same level as the misty-diamond-engagement-ring adverts that trade on the word 'forever'. Such romanticism makes all things palatable, and fixes life firmly on the other side of our own selfish fence.

This fixing, or stereotyping, is at the heart of romance, putting men and women into roles based upon economics. Women are feminine and men are masculine (or passive and dominant respectively) and no psychological complexity is allowed to blur the clarity of that demarcation. If it were . . . then men might start hating the image of themselves disguished as cars or cigars or movie stars; and women might just reject the romantic appeal of perfume, After Eight mints, and sparkling kitchen floors, and then the whole consumer edifice would collapse. Who then would have the money for *Penthouse*, or Mills and Boon and Cartland? Romance is part of the establishment, founded upon good commercial sense.

'Human kind cannot bear very much reality', wrote T. S. Eliot. And yet to take the leap and nod, condescendingly, that romance does no harm to all the foolish women who read it, is to undervalue the power of words. If good literature has the power to change the inner world for the better, to enlarge, to instil compassion, then who is to say that romance does not corrupt?

If more and more women buy the books and believe even a part of all the romantic nonsense, then there is a danger that they will expect too much . . . that it *should* all be happy ever after, as of right.

This spring, the couples will get married, in love, as they have always done, and we know from statistics and experience that one out of three of those marriages will break up, a brutal end to all the expectations of romance. Some of the break-ups will happen because it was not as they had hoped, not so sexy, not so romantic, and they could not stand the disappointment.

But some of the couples will discover the limitations of romance at last. They will stop being 'in love', find sex monotonous after a while, like eating the same meal day after day, fantasize about other people, discover that dirty nappies have nothing to do with the desirable images that sell babyfood and washing powder, and they will look at each other and notice frowns and wrinkles.

And – here is the miracle of the imagination that is truly Romantic but has nothing to do with romance – they will, gradually, begin to love each other. Love – there is a word to relish. Love respects those parts of the other which are awkward and unstereotyped and embraces them. It recognizes that the love of partner, children, and old parents has to do with a precious and wearisome sense of responsibility, lighter for being reciprocated.

It knows that death makes the 'forever' a lie, and (perhaps because of that) it laughs at passion and raises kindness, patience, tolerance and humour upon a chipped pedestal. It values cuddles as much as sex, ceasing to see the fat thighs, balding head, crowsfeet, reaching for the whole person. Romance is an illusion, but love is born through a million little disillusionments, and does not grow on a tropical island, nor a misty heath, nor a passionate honeymoon bed, nor in red roses . . . but meekly and bravely in your own back yard.

Photographer as Recidivist

It is easy to recall the very moment when photography was tricked out as art, not by Cartier-Bresson, but by a click of East Enders with Nikons. Reality was distorted by the fish-eye lens, the most indifferent head-shot could be close-cropped and claim 'character', and even good magazines like *Nova* would splash a neatly-focused elbow across two pages and call it a fashion photograph. The black and white was moody, and you measured life by a shutter-speed . . . then in the heady Sixties and Seventies when Terence Donovan and David Bailey were followed by a thousand little snappers who saved up for Prakticas and portfolios, and lusted for a by-line.

Bailey, as we know, appointed himself guardian of the ikons. Years later, Donovan has allowed a collection of his 'work' to be published, the use of the word itself implying the weight of art, of *oeuvre*, rather than simple graft. A lavish volume called *Glances* is his testament to 'the evaporative qualities of human life'. The photographs are technically good (but then, given the sophistication of equipment, it would be astonishing if they were not) and even moderately inventive (although the image of girl-sloughing-tulle-on-bed captioned by irrelevant hobby details was perfected by *Penthouse* long ago), whilst paper and printing are first-class. The whole product is a convincing exposé of photography as over-rated craft, and of successful photographer as recidivist, committing his little habitual crimes against good taste.

Donovan's first offence is against language. The images are obvious enough; sprawling thighs, black stockings and suspenders, soapsuds, with the fantasy of policewoman-whore thrown in, or rather *up*. Mercifully, there are few words, but the few crack under the strain. 'If there is a street, there will be people moving through it and across it, vehicles passing either fast or slow down it. I ask you to consider the notion that none of those objects, people or vehicles will ever re-form in that precise order again that you are now observing them'. A snap of a naked girl is captioned: 'Thinking of success, fame, security, failure, love. All these things cascade through her conscience like escaped mercury'. Whether or not the movement of mercury can be described with precision by that verb or not, one might have expected the publishers to discourage Mr Donovan from omitting full stops at the end of all his captions. It is slow-speed pretension.

His second offence is more serious; against truth. One example suffices, a snap of a water-spattered black body with this caption: 'She is a genuine African princess. She yearns to go back but the political police are waiting. Such a sweet, cheery girl, but you can't tell how sweet her smile was'. Yet Donovan introduces the collection by stating that the snaps are 'reconstructed moments that escaped my camera'. So *is* this an African princess, or not? If not (as we must believe) then what possible justification can there be for the tasteless-ness of the caption, and for cropping off that 'sweet smile'. An alleged maid from Manila also appears in the guise of a grass-skirted rump, and the caption informs us that this is another example of homesick Third World woman glad to lose face – for Terry.

Oh but faces, faces belong to *people*, and lead us to the third offence. These are obviously photographs of women; they are not pictures of people. It is possible to view poorly-focused legs and buttocks, and read the caption, 'Jamaica. What jiggling, wriggling people live there. Smells, burning leaves . . .' and laugh with the generous assumption that he is sending himself up. It is equally possible to flick through the snaps of headless torsos, sigh that soft-porn should still be peddled in the name of art, and dismiss it as old-fashioned nonsense: a fossil from the Meafterall Age. The third option is to question, again, the effect of such glamourizing of soft-porn stereotypes.

It is interesting how the censorship debate has moved, since the days when we danced to the tune of 'Anything Goes' and joined the Defence of Literature and the Arts Society. Feminists (who would once have rejected the Whitehouse/Holbrook lobby) were the first to mutter, to question the freedom to show women as objects of humiliation and abuse. It is a long way from Donovan to a snuff movie, and yet what, after all, is the essence of the headless torso? It is dehumanized, divested of essential identity, transformed into chunks of meat. The photographer, or television documentary maker, who allows his camera to linger thus, without questioning, is no different from the itchy little man who stuffs his 50p into the slot of a Soho peepshow. It is not possible now, as it once was, to assert that the visual image does not harm. Its significance is indissoluble from a cultural history which ranges from the religious image, the icon, to the glossiest commercial hard-sell.

So the argument went, and still goes on, for these are serious times. Donovan will protest that he is only trying to bring a little fantasy and fun into people's lives. But who *are* these people? In any case, I have a little fantasy of my own. I am having a bath in this horse-chestnut gelée that promises anything can happen, when wham! who should come through the window but Mr Donovan waving his *enormous* telephoto. He tells me to smile cheerily; but this time the torso-shot and the caption are mine: 'Studio. Bathtime. What thoughts of life rocket through his brain like exploding microbes! He wanted to study philosophy and painting but he ended up a photographer. Who is to know what he might have been. A poor heavy-goods vehicle, perhaps.'

Beowulf—
A Reassessment

(Spectator 1982)

It is not perhaps the most attractive of poems, and certainly not accessible. Those two negatives would matter only if you expect literature to be easy on the eye and the mind; paradoxically, they unite to give the greatest Anglo-Saxon poem its weird (*wyrd*: fate) power. For that distant land is mist-wreathed and hostile, peopled by inarticulate warriors and beasts beyond human imagining, and the language echoes in its bleak caverns, harsh and guttural. In its original form *Beowulf* clangs with the barbaric beauty of a Sutton Hoo shield; in translation it conveys a powerful sense of desolation. Few things in literature can equal the simple, unequivocal dignity with which the hero (he with the handgrip of thirty men, but doomed as all men are doomed) introduces himself: 'Beowulf is min nama.' There is simultaneous madness, pathos and pride in his acceptance of whatever horror will befall him: 'Gæð a wyrd swa hio scel' (fate goes ever as it must).

I have not always shown such enthusiasm. In 1967, a student at University College London, I was vociferous (and fashionable) in my complaints about Anglo Saxon, then a compulsory part of the syllabus. Absenting myself from Professor Randolph Quirk's lectures, I proclaimed (with an ignorance as deep as Grendel's swamp) that *Beowulf* was a waste of time; this was a parroting of the more general demand at the tail-end of the Sixties that our university studies should be 'relevant' – as if all art should be confined within the tiny tenement of one's narrow, individual experience.

Egocentricity, laziness, and lack of literary judgement aside, a more fundamental historical error lurked at the heart of that demand. It was the assumption that the twentieth century has a unique insight into alienation and despair, and even anger against any implacable 'system'. So Albert Camus, Robert Lowell, and Sylvia Plath were placed on their pedestals, and whilst William Blake might be revered for his 'revolutionary' ideas, most of the 'Eng.Lit.' syllabus was doomed to be studied as a task rather than a pleasure. It was strange that Ted Hughes's savage monsters should have been so avidly accepted by a generation which made an easy cult of Tolkien, and yet saw the monster Grendel, his awful mother and the Dragon, as dull – or (at best) of mere philological interest.

Such shibboleths would not bear repetition, were it not for the fact that they have become absorbed by a system of state education which threw out Latin from comprehensive schools, thus denying 'ordinary' children access to the language of power, of nuance, of myth. The protests of my generation of students ensured that Anglo Saxon met a similar fate within the universities, becoming an option few would choose. By the time I reached my final year, forced to read the texts if I wanted a degree, I was willing to suspect that I might have been wrong. The *Battle of Maldon*, the *Dream of the Rood*, *Wanderer* and *Seafarer*, and most of all *Beowulf* have all taught me what I then guessed but have since known to be true: first, what W. B. Yeats called correctly 'the fascination of what's difficult'; and second, the spiritual relevance (no other word will do) of those earliest of English poems.

Beowulf, a hero of the Geatish people, crosses the sea to rid the Danish king of the hideous monster, Grendel, who has invaded his hall at night to devour his men. Eschewing weapons, Beowulf kills Grendel with his bare hands, and later the creature's mother suffers the same fate in her underwater lair. Many years later Beowulf, now king of his people, kills a Dragon who guards a hoard of treasure, dies of his wounds, and is buried on a high promontory overlooking the sea. That is all that happens. The modern reader may feel revulsion at the poem's relentlessness, the sense that man has no choices, caught up in implacable fate. Yet though dark fate is the abstract motif, it can also be seen that Beowulf contributes to his own destruction, the epic hero attaining the far more interesting status of tragic hero. For he dies with his eyes upon the gold-hoard of the dragon, which is identified by Tolkien as 'a personification of malice, greed, destruction (the evil side of heroic life) and of the undiscriminating cruelty of fortune that distinguishes not good or bad'. His loyal retainers, silenced by the death of greatness, bury their king, and the poet comments: 'They . . . left the gold in the ground where it still exists, as unprofitable to men as it had been before'. That moral insight, and the subtle adjectives used to describe Beowulf in the closing lines ('the mildest and gentlest of men, the kindest to his people and most eager for praise') should banish the notion that *Beowulf* is a barbarous relic of an alien age. Its perceptions are universal, and the American poet Richard Wilbur has encapsulated the thoroughly 'modern', though poignant, isolation of its hero:

> *He died in his own country a kinless king,*
> *A name heavy with deeds, and mourned as one*
> *Will mourn for the frozen year when it is done.*
> *They buried him next the sea on a thrust of land:*
> *Twelve men rode round his barrow all in a ring,*
> *Singing of him what they could understand.*

There is an image from the Anglo-Saxon world, recorded in Bede, which, in its simplicity, conveys the particular power of this literature. A sparrow is flying through the night, through the stormy darkness. Suddenly it chances to encounter the

209

open eaves of a great warrior-hall, and for a few seconds it experiences the light, the warmth, the noise all around it. Then the bird flies out through the opening on the opposite side, and continues its trackless journey through the icy darkness: 'So is the life of man revealed for a brief space, but what went before and what follows we know not.'

For the anonymous authors of *Beowulf* and the other poems, the image of the sparrow was a metaphor for life itself: a few seconds of joy surrounded by harsh nothingness. Since man was doomed to die, by age, illness, or violence, he had to do his utmost to ensure that his 'fame' would live, and there was desperation as well as glory in that heroism: the struggle with whatever metaphorical monsters might cross one's path. Chaucer's jovial pilgrims set out in Spring under a curved dome of sky that certainly contained their God, and they were assured of their place in the Great Chain of Being. The *Beowulf* poet had no such faith: only a sense of wintry inevitability and a foreboding of doom, both of which find an echo in this century in the work of Thomas Hardy.

The Anglo-Saxon sparrow is first cousin to the Darkling Thrush, an inhabitant of a familiar bleak landscape who carries with him, nevertheless, an intimation of joy. The light and warmth may last but a few seconds, but they are there for all that. The prevailing mood may be elegaic, but regret and rejoining are two sides of the same coin: the knowledge that all things pass and yet are the more precious because threatened by darkness. The poet celebrates human life and nature in all its brevity: the sun on the *swan-rad* (swan-road, sea), the freshness of wind in the sails, the shimmer of welcoming cliffs, the loyalty of friends, the exercise of virtues, the sense of carving out achievement in the short, allotted time.

Centuries separate this glorious and melancholy poem from the life I lead. Yet its language is my own, its hero is incarnate upon my horizon, its vision of the struggle between good and evil maintains its truth, and all its preoccupations are mine. For me *Beowulf* is yet another moving testimony to man's ability to *make* joy within the seethe of chaos, vanquishing the Dragon.